PROJECT

A Rites of Passage Program

Philosophy, Theory, and Overview

By
Joe Benton, Derrick Jackson,
and Burnett Gallman

Introduction by
Anthony T. Browder, Author of *From the Browder File Vols. I & 2, Nile Valley Contributions to Civilization*

Copyright 2022 by Joe Benton, Derrick Jackson, and Burnett Gallman

No part of this publication may be reproduced or transmitted in any form or by any electronic or mechanical means, including but not limited to photocopying, xerographic printing, electronic information storage and retrieval systems, and/or keying into any form of magnetic media storage and retrieval systems, without written permission from the authors.

ISBN: 9781735974972

For information about this publication or **Project: Sankofa,** write to:

Imhotep-The Drum
P.O. Box 290778
Columbia, South Carolina 29229

About the cover:

The cover is a reproduction of a print entitled "Home, Sweet, Home..." by Damond L. Howard of Awendaw, South Carolina. Mr. Howard has been an artist since the age of six. He attended South Carolina State University, where he earned a Bachelor of Science degree in Art Education. He continues to produce art in various mediums and teaches in a high school in Charleston, South Carolina.

For information about the cover art, write to:
Damond L. Howard,
1036 Gadsenville Road,
Awendaw, South Carolina 29429

Printed in the United States of America

Dedication (Second Edition)

This effort is dedicated to our brother, friend, and co-writer, Joe E. Benton (Maa Kheru), now an esteemed Ancestor. He is sorely missed.

Dedication (First Edition)

For our Afrikan Ancestors who left a blueprint for us to follow. They left challenges for us, the most difficult being to match their wisdom and spirituality in today's material world.

Also, for our youth, without whom there is no future. They give us the reason to continue to fight the, sometimes absurd, battles in which we find ourselves embroiled.

Acknowledgements

We would like to first thank the Creator, without whom nothing is possible.

We also, profoundly and gratefully, thank our families who did without their husbands and fathers during the process of writing this book and also during the training experiences that led to the formation of these books. We thank them for their timely suggestions, criticisms, and observations. To Almateen, Joe III, and Adia, Yvonne and Tiye, Jodi and Khali…We love you dearly!!! Thanks also to Mrs. Arlonial D. Bradford, Gerald Jones, Wilma King, and Marguerite (Aunt M.L.) Delaine for their timely critiques.

We'd also like to thank the staff at the former St. Luke's Center for their dedication to our youth, including and especially Victor Roberts and Theresa Weldon. Their love for and sincere dedication to the uplift of our youth is truly inspiring.

Much appreciation to Marian David, Olive Wright Covington, the staff at the Children's Defense Fund, and Gloria Purvis with Dyer's Hill African Methodist Episcopal Zion Church, Bennettsville, South Carolina, for giving us the opportunity, challenge, and freedom to show the positive results of this program.

Thanks also to Sister Jocelyn Clarkson for her time, her patience, and for challenging us through her questions.

Profound thanks to Mrs. Toretha Wright, who patiently edited this second edition and sympathetically empathized with our hesitations after the transition of our brother, Joe Benton (Maa Kheru).

We'd like to thank Dr. Marimba Ani for taking the time to review the original document. Her suggestions were and are greatly appreciated.

Last but not least, many thanks to the Thursday Morning Breakfast Brotherhood (now Saturday afternoon brunch), who challenged us with ideas, and to the Nzinga Study group of ASCAC (especially the sisters), who kept us thinking.

Table of Contents

Dedication (Second Edition)

Dedication (First Edition)

Acknowledgements

Introduction i

Project Sankofa: A Rites of Passage Program

Authors' Introduction v

Nothing Just Happens

PART I - Plain Language Overview of Rites of Passage

Project Sankofa Defined 1

Afrikan Centered Rites of Passage 3

Goals and Objectives of an Afrikan Centered Rites of Passage Program 6

The Rites of Passage Movement 9

How to Choose A Rites of Passage Program 11

Structure of a Rites of Passage Program 17

The Importance of Ritual 18

PART II - The Philosophy Behind The Structural Units

Unit One "Yes, I'm Bad" 27

Unit Two "Not that Black Stuff Again" 48

Unit Three "We'll Learn Ya,' Durn Ya" 65

Unit Four "Making the Right Choices" 87

Unit Five "I've Got a Plan" 97

Unit Six "Being Poor Ain't No Virtue" 102

Unit Seven "Ebonically Speaking" 115

Unit Eight "To Be Healthy or Not to Be" 137

Bibliography and Suggested Reading for Project Sankofa 163

Glossary: Words to Guide You Home: A Journey of Self Discovery 176

Appendix A

Black Men on Which to Do Biographical Research 209

Appendix B

Black Women on Which to Do Biographical Research... 211

Appendix C

Proverbs that can be used in Rites of Passage Programs 213

Appendix D

List of Words, Phrases, and Concepts 217

About the Authors 221

Introduction

Project Sankofa: A Rites of Passage Program

To some, life is a mystery filled with numerous obstacles and challenges which can cause the most promising individuals to become confused and lose their direction. To others, life is a journey full of mysteries, obstacles, and challenges that are minimized because they possess a map that leads them to their final destination with minimum confusion and delay.

Without second-guessing, it is easy to predict that those who are guided through life will be more accomplished than those who are not. Successful people ensure the success of future generations by guiding youth through life and pointing out difficulties to be avoided. Those youth without proper guidance wander aimlessly through life and seldom achieve their highest potential. A philosopher expressed this reality quite poetically by saying, "Life is involved in both perpetuating itself and surpassing itself, and if all life does is maintain itself - then living is only not dying."

Within American society, Europeans have retained their power by perpetuating cultural traditions, which ensured that each generation would surpass the accomplishments of their ancestors. Conversely, Afrikans in America have maintained positions of relative powerlessness because their cultural traditions have been stripped, outlawed, and rendered undesirable by the dominant power holders. Afrikans will remain powerless and in survival mode as long as they remain detached from cultural traditions, which teach them to love themselves and adopt meaningful values.

European values are not Afrikan values. *Project Sankofa: A Rites of Passage Program* makes the distinctions perfectly clear. The pathways to social, financial, and spiritual empowerment for Afrikan people are distinctly different from European pathways. *Project Sankofa: A Rites of Passage Program*, tells us what these differences are, thereby, making it easier to apply sound judgment. It's like placing a clean glass next to a dirty one.

The historical and philosophical lessons in *Project Sankofa: A Rites of Passage Program* are more than stories written to make Afrikans feel good about themselves. The Nguzo Saba, Principles of Maat, Declarations of Innocence, and 10 Virtues, are cardinal points on a moral compass, that will direct Afrikan people to the path of righteousness. The Afrikan-centered approaches to economics, communication, decision making, health, and hygiene offer valuable insights into aspects of life that make Afrikan people whole again.

The perspectives offered by brothers Benton, Jackson, and Gallman must be studied and implemented if youth are to be guided from adolescence to adulthood with minimum loss of life. For our youth live in a world where decadence and self-centeredness are the acceptable norms. In this world, it is commonplace for youth to kill one another over tennis shoes and petty disagreements or for manhood and womanhood to be determined by the number of children conceived without proper planning. These are the accepted norms for members of a sick society. Acceptance of these sick modes of nonthinking and outrageous behavior dooms one to become a permanent member of the social and economic underclass. To cure this sickness, sometimes drastic but always realistic measures need to be taken.

Project Sankofa: A Rites of Passage Program is about going back and reclaiming the traditions of the past in order to establish new standards of normalcy. A paradigm shift is required, and it must begin in the minds of the youth, who will be given new standards of excellence to model. Rites of Passage programs are designed to accomplish that objective.

Such ideas, however, will appear strange to a people who have been conditioned to reject their past and now live precariously in the present moment. Such ideas will be rejected by those lacking understanding of Afrikan culture. These fears must not stand in the way of the work being done to enhance the lives of current and future generations of Afrikan youth.

We owe it to our ancestors to reclaim the valued traditions of the past, and in doing so, we honor ourselves. We owe it to our descendants to light the path that they must walk, and in doing so, we honor ourselves. We owe it to our descendants to light the path that they must walk, and in doing so, we honor our ancestors. The ancestors, ourselves, and our descendants are all part of a spiritual circle held together by the bonds of cultural continuity. Rites of Passages are the crucibles in which those bonds are forged and dispersed throughout the generations.

Project Sankofa: A Rites of Passage Program is a noble and honorable work and must be added to the growing list of documents that comprise the current Afrikan renaissance. I am proud to give my support to this project and encourage everyone to do the same. Let us now begin the work, which will long be remembered as a major turning point in the history of Afrikan people.

Anthony T. Browder, author of *From the Browder File, Volumes I and II* and *Exploding the Myths, Volume I: Nile Valley Contributions to Civilization*

Authors' Introduction

Nothing Just Happens

Each generation must, out of relative obscurity, discover its mission and, having discovered it, either betray or fulfill it.
- Franz Fanon

One of the most influential books/studies ever written about Americans of Afrikan descent was *An American Dilemma: The Negro Problem and Modern Democracy*. This study, undertaken by the Swedish researcher, Gunnar Myrdal, was funded by the Carnegie Corporation. It was originally published in 1944, but a revised edition was distributed in 1962. The book contained over 1500 pages and spoke to nearly every issue confronting Afrikans in America. This book was credited with influencing the decision of the United States Supreme Court in rendering its decision in the 1954 desegregation case, "Brown vs. The Board of Education," which, in effect, eliminated legal "separate but equal" conditions in schools and, later, in other public facilities.

Several interesting facets of the book bear close study. The first is its insightfulness on the impact of systematic discrimination and racism in the United States. The other facets relate to the solutions posed by Myrdal. The most revealing conclusion is discussed in Chapter 7, entitled "Population." On page 167, this statement appears:

"There is no doubt that the overwhelming majority of white Americans desire that there be as few Negroes as possible in America. If the Negro could be eliminated from America. If the Negro could be eliminated from America or greatly decreased in numbers, this would meet the white's approval

- provided that it could be accomplished by means, which are also approved. Correspondingly, an increase of the proportion of Negroes in the American population is commonly looked upon as undesirable."

(The theme of how to get rid of Afrikans in America is revisited brilliantly in the short story "The Space Traders" by Derrick Bell in his provocative book, *Faces at the Bottom of the Well: The Permanence of Racism* (BasicBooks, NY, 1992).)

Myrdal went on to discuss various approaches to this "elimination," which included the wholesale slaughter of Negroes (he termed this approach unacceptable in light of general public reaction to such a solution being used in Germany against Jews). He agreed that the "elimination" should be done slowly but ruled out mass deportation and overt denial of health care. Of interest is his conclusion that controlling the fertility of Afrikan people was the method of choice.

He also concluded that the only Americans who believed in the "American Dream" were Negroes. No other racial group wanted the melting pot theory to work for all, except when it benefited their kind.

While being hailed as a "liberal" document, this study was the basis of a plan which underlies many of the problems faced in the African community today. Every weakness of what was then called the "Negro" community was discussed, and options were presented.

Daily events occur because someone wants them to occur. Further, someone benefits from these events. The expressed goal of this study was to discover a humane-appearing method of elimination of people of Afrikan descent from America. The terrible shape in which we find our children, our families, and our community is due to an intentional sequence of events, a specifically designed plan. That specific design is based upon valuation (a sociological term for how things ought to be). The approach used is called socialization.

Afrikan children in America are socialized to do poorly scholastically and to behave poorly. General expectation levels are low for most Afrikan children. This socialization process is best seen in schools. Our children are doing poorly in school, both academically and behaviorally. If one boy or girl is doing poorly, we can conclude that something may be wrong with that child. However, if you review the local, state, or national statistics on misbehavior or academic performance, you will find that Afrikan boys and girls rank highest in areas of poor performance regardless of the location. If we understand the concept of "nothing just happens," then we realize that educational programs are designed and put together in such a way as to result in failure for Afrikan children. Therefore, it seems logical that there is nothing wrong with our children. The system is just designed to victimize them.

Demanding that a system (which is designed to be detrimental to our children) successfully educates or socializes our children is an effort in futility. The system is supposed to make failures of our children. You may ask, why is this so? You may even attempt to refute the argument detailed herein. However, if you look realistically at the statistics and look carefully around you, these very strong statements cannot be summarily dismissed. We must come to the realization that the American systems of education, economics, and socialization were never designed to benefit Afrikan people. Yet, we have deluded ourselves into believing that it should work for us.

Most people immigrating to this country have done so either to escape from oppressive systems in their home countries or to look for better lives than they could find in their home countries. Most of these immigrants have believed that they would have religious, economic, political, and social freedom in America. The literature, education, history, constitution, and propaganda of America speak to this very issue. However, in reviewing religious, economic, political, social, and propaganda data, there is no mention of such rationales for immigration for most people of Afrikan descent. In fact, even in situations where Afrikans want to immigrate to America in order to flee an oppressive system, they are not welcome (such as the people from Haiti).

The overwhelming majority of people of Afrikan descent did not originally come to this country seeking any of the freedoms sought by others. The vast majority of Afrikans came here enslaved to work for and benefit others (with no compensation). The impact of this difference has had a profound effect on the psyche of people of Afrikan descent even today.

Clearly stated, Afrikan people did not ask to be here, and when they did come, it was to serve. Bring that mindset to the present and consider that one of the myths surrounding Afrikans is that they lack motivation. Since the reason for being here was different, then it should be expected that the motivation should be different from those who came for other reasons. Additionally, all other people came with their culture and cultural identities intact, whereas Afrikan people were denied that linkage, primarily by force. Afrikans were brought into an environment where Afrikan culture, religion, and history were systematically removed from their knowledge base. Since the process of socialization calls for culture and history to be a part of the knowledge base, Afrikans were forced to imitate and take as their own the culture and history of others (who were enslaving, oppressing, and hating them).

The second part of the mindset dealt with serving others. Slavery is an economic system. Afrikans were enslaved and brought to the Americas to underpin the economic system. At the initial start of the "New World", free labor made economic profit a foregone conclusion. The profit derived from the enslavement of Afrikan people made Americans and America very rich. This material wealth was flaunted in the face of Afrikans while they were enslaved and later after they were "freed." Once they were "freed," wealth was, and is, used as a measuring stick for success. Yet, the periods of overt enslavement, segregation, and discrimination are conveniently forgotten when success equations are developed.

The avenues for achieving appropriate motivation and obtaining the desired material goods of life in America have been blocked. The attempt to navigate these avenues has been a source of constant trouble, struggle, denial, and self-hatred for the Afrikans who survived the Maafa and for their descendants. Achieving more than just survival has been a source of tremendous frustration for many, if not most Afrikans in America. "Success" for many has been and is measured by material wealth and the imitation of the lifestyles and behavior of other cultures, especially that of European cultures. The closer one comes to approximating the traits of others, the greater is the separation from self and from those who resemble self. Also, the more successful he or she is likely to be. Thus, we are rewarded (although superficially) for contributing to our own cultural destruction. Unfortunately, in accepting the "hype" of materialism, too many of us do not understand (or care) what we are doing to our Ancestors or descendants.

Who benefits from this process? Though this question has many answers, only a limited number will be discussed here. As long as we remember that "nothing just happens" and that there is a plan at work with a definite goal, we can reason together in order to obtain some of the answers.

America, with the exception of agriculture, is no longer a producing nation. Slaves, indentured servants, and large numbers of unskilled and/or manual laborers are no longer necessary. The vast number of Afrikans, who filled these positions in the past, are a useless resource pool. However, many people of European descent are also not needed. One solution has been to develop a service industry, prisons, wherein Afrikans can reside and Europeans can be employed. Please note that the prison industry is the fastest growing industry in America. This strategy has produced low unemployment for the unskilled European labor force and high detention rates for people of Afrikan descent. Please review arrest, detention, incarceration, length of detention, and crime rates in the National Uniform Crime Reports and note that the crime rates are about the same for nearly all communities. Anyone should be able to obtain a Uniform Crime Reports book by contacting the justice department in Washington, DC. However, if we look at what happens after arrest, we get different data. A little personal research may reveal some interesting facts to you, but what should be kept in mind is the ultimate goal.

The eugenics goal of involuntary sterilization and birth control focused on Afrikan communities was an effort to achieve reduction in birth rates. One way to slowly eliminate Afrikans in America is to reduce birth rates. Reduction of birth rates would not be done voluntarily unless a method of separating fertile males from fertile females could be found. Then the ultimate goal of reducing birth rates could be realized.

Prison has become the justifiable means to achieve the goal. There also have been many spill-over "benefits," such as low marriage rates and the breakdown of many Afrikan families. The newest wrinkle is to make prison guards of Afrikan women while squeezing them off welfare. One must look at the big picture; Afrikan men are criminalized and incarcerated out of proportion to European Americans who commit the same crimes, then Afrikan wives, mothers, sisters, and daughters are being paid to keep them incarcerated and under "control." Have you ever caught yourself saying, "What's wrong with our people?" It is all part of a design.

Nothing just happens! Current events are designed to benefit the society based upon the valuation goals of that society. Since nothing just happens, it is imperative that life-giving and life-sustaining strategies be developed within Afrikan communities in America. One such strategy is provided in how we have socialized our children. They must be socialized to succeed while being themselves and not imitating others. In order for this to occur, they must be socialized to solve problems and view the world from an Afrikan worldview and from an Afrikan context.

If this sounds preachy to you, you are right. For we cannot expect others to do for us what we are unwilling to do for ourselves. Afrikan children remaining and acting like children well into their thirties and forties is not only the problem of society but also the problem of our community. In fact, the "larger" (European-American) community benefits when our children's immaturity involves actions that result in legal consequences. That our children are not learning is not the problem of schools in our society, the problem is our unwillingness to develop schools to provide the results we want. When our children become juvenile delinquents, it is not the problem of society's police or court systems, it is our lack of instilling an Afrikan value system in them (our children). We should have known for years that America was not designed for us or our benefit. Yet, we are still here and have yet to develop a system within this system to benefit all of us.

Rites of Passage is, however, a system that, when used with our children and supported by adults, makes American systems user-friendly. The methods of this approach are based on the reality of human socialization. Other approaches have not worked for us because they were not designed for us and by us. Nothing just happens! Rites of Passage programs demand the best from Afrikan people, and there is positive growth. Both the instructors and trainees are changed and affected by the challenges presented by the program. The changes are positive, thought-provoking, and, in many instances, immediate.

As the prison populations have risen, so has the call for Rites of Passage programs (nothing just happens). The key concepts found in most Afrikan Centered approaches and those that have had the highest positive impact involve the following:

Positive Self Concept

A combination of self-esteem, identity, purpose, and direction for one's life. It is important to differentiate between self-concept, which is how one sees oneself, and self-esteem, which is how one feels about oneself.

Afrikan History, Philosophy, and Culture

Understanding oneself through connecting with the past and the past's relationship to the present and to the future.

Afrikan Education

The utilization of not only the work of great achievers but the understanding of the lasting achievement of Afrikan people. This includes creating an understanding of the need for and use of value systems.

Problem Solving and Decision Making

Learning and using ancient methods to resolve life's pressing problems and teaching trainees how to think as opposed to what to think.

Collective Economics

Learning to pool financial and material resources to benefit the entire community.

Community, Art, and Aesthetic Skills

Learning to use talents of intuition, art, and speaking for increased understanding. Also, learning to recognize and neutralize the traps laid for us in the popular media. In this vein, please note that the word "Afrika" and its derivatives are spelled with a "k" instead of a "c" in keeping with the general linguistic rules of most Afrikan languages.

Health, Hygiene Sciences

Teaching trainees the essentials of health and practices to avoid as related to personal and community health. Also, teaching trainees the scientific heritage of African People.

This is a work in progress. While we lean heavily on information relating to Afrikan people, we realize that while we are indeed, Afrikan people, we have become another ethnic group, the Ausa people (Afrikans in the United States of America). Therefore, we have adapted some information to fit our particular environmental circumstances.

This is a tried-and-true program. Using this theoretical background, we have been fortunate enough to positively influence many young women and men over the years.

The mastery of these essential qualities increases the value of the individual, not just to self, but to the entire community. These lessons will not happen unless the community wants them to happen. There are two paths that the Afrikan community can take. One path is to quietly follow the trail of tears and destruction while adhering to the goals of others and be eliminated slowly. The other path is to continually work with and improve upon Rites of Passage programs to save us from the planned destruction. Remember, nothing just happens.

When I was a child, I spake as a child, I understood as a child, I thought as a child: but when I became a man, I put away childish things.

I Corinthians 13:11, *The Bible, KJV*

PART I

Plain Language Overview of Rites of Passage

Project Sankofa Defined

Sankofa is a word taken from the Adinkra symbology of the Akan people of Ghana that literally means, "Go back and fetch it." This infers that in order to have a meaningful future, we must thoroughly understand our past. One Sankofa symbol is that of a bird with its body facing one way and its head turned backward, cleaning its feathers. The feathers should be clean before they can fly. Our Ausa Ancestors said that one does not give bricks to those who would fly, but it is the responsibility of the Elders to help those who would fly with their flight plans. The other Sankofa symbol looks like a fancy stylized heart. It is a symbol that most Americans have seen in that it was originally placed in the ironworks that our enslaved Ancestors were forced to create, especially in Southern coastal regions like Charleston and Beaufort, SC, Savannah, GA, Mobile, AL, and New Orleans, LA. It was a message to us, their descendants waning us not to forget our past and beseeching us not to forget them and their sufferings.

Project Sankofa is a coming together of Afrikan Centered men and women dedicated to guiding and developing Afrikan boys and girls (who reside in America) to true manhood and womanhood. It is the merging of three organizations in Columbia, South Carolina, Imhotep Enterprises, St. Luke's Life Skills Center, and A Concerned Group of Men. Using various methods, these organizations provided Afrikan Centered and comprehensive training programs for almost ten years. These organizations combined forces and techniques more than 20 years ago and evolved into Project: Sankofa.

Many of the early graduates of the programs are now alumni of many colleges and universities, such as Ivy League schools and especially Historically Black Colleges and Universities (HBCUs). Some of the graduates were counted among the leaders of their middle schools, high schools, and colleges. The only real differences were the histories of the participants. The boys and girls ranged from seriously delinquent offenders to students with good grades to the devoutly religious. The results have been the same for all three groups. At least three of the delinquent offenders became Class Presidents at their respective schools. The good students continued to excel, and the religious students were even more deeply involved in their respective religious activities. We are proud to have participated in the production of genuinely good people who are concerned with the betterment of their communities.

Project Sankofa is one of the oldest and most continuous manhood and womanhood (Rites of Passage) training programs in the United States. Though most of our efforts at providing Rites of Passage programs have been in South Carolina, the impact of Project Sankofa has extended to many other states through correspondence, training workshops, and the movement of the young people who complete the program. The focus of the founders of Project Sankofa now, is to train trainers in the provision of Rites of Passage programs that can be replicated by the new trainers at their home organizations and communities.

Afrikan Centered Rites of Passage

"African Americans must forsake the white man's social structures, concepts of justice and yes, even religion and return, as far as possible, to the genuine African values and identity (insofar as these can be accurately recovered and reconstituted)."

Michael Bradley, *Chosen People from the Caucasus* Chicago: Third World Press, 2013

To be Afrikan Centered means that one processes all information from the perspective of being an Afrikan person. This analysis ultimately means that a person of Afrikan origin has correctly identified her/himself and has placed her/himself in an appropriate frame of reference. It means that the person of Afrikan origin does not see her/himself from the perspective of other non-Afrikan people. An Afrikan Centered person does not necessarily reject other non-Afrikan schools of thought but is able to process them externally rather than internally.

Afrikan Centered thinking uses a core of Afrikan culture and philosophy. The Afrikan Centered individual attempts to understand Afrikan culture and philosophy before being altered by the Arabs and the Europeans. Once a degree of understanding is achieved, these disciplines can be applied to the present in order to forge a future that will be positive for all people, but especially for people of Afrikan origin. The idea is not to blindly chase things believed to be Afrikan. We must be able to pick out those things that are appropriate to us and throw out those things that are not useful.

There have been several successful Afrikan Centered Rites of Passage Programs in the United States. Several of these programs are the Sons of Afrika in New York City with Dr. Leonard Jeffries and Prof. James Small, the H.A.W.K. Program in California with Doctors Lawford Goddard and

Wade W. Nobles, Prof. Paul Hill's Rites of Passage Programs in Ohio, Let the Circle Be Unbroken in Memphis, Tennessee with Dr. Theresa Okwumabua and Project Sankofa in South Carolina. Additionally, several renowned scholars, Dr. Marimba Ani, Dr. Asa Hilliard, Doctors Nathan and Julia Hare, Dr. Leonard Jeffries, Prof. James Small, and Brother Anthony T. Browder (to name a few) are involved with or have called for continuous Rites of Passage Programs in their communities and in their published works.

African Centered programs are developed using modernized ancient Afrikan principles, strategies, techniques, and cultural practices in creating conscious, competent, and committed adults. In the past, in most Afrikan ethnic groups, Rites of Passage programs and ceremonies have been the glue that connected the generations of the society together. After the Europeans conquered Afrika, they (usually missionaries and teachers) declared war on Afrikan culture. Rites of Passage customs were called names like "heathen," "pagan," and "barbaric," and were strongly discouraged. As a result of this pressure, unfortunately, there are some ethnic groups in Afrika who have apparently lost all memory of Rites of Passage ceremonies (e.g., the Ga in Ghana).

The use of European culture and concepts have had little, if any, positive effect on children of Afrikan descent despite being repackaged and changed in different situations. Actually, it is questionable if European culture, values, and other concepts have had a positive effect even on children of European descent. Traditionally, European culture has been relatively *user-unfriendly* regarding the treatment of children and childrearing patterns. In the development of positive self-concepts, the Afrikan approach uses core Afrikan philosophies, as will be demonstrated more fully later. European culture, as practiced in the United States, denies the self-worth of Afrikans and for centuries has sought to destroy

Afrikan and other cultures. Although many European-based programs are well-meaning in their efforts to work with Afrikan children, these programs can only inherently alienate an Afrikan child from himself or herself. Within European culture, there were and are no positive models of Afrika or of Afrikan people.

European culture has, however, made some meritorious progress in the area of technology. For Afrikans to flourish, they will have to master the use of technology. European culture, however, has serious flaws in the areas of ethics, sociology, psychology, and metaphysics. In these areas of human interaction, the European is the least civilized of all cultures on the planet. We must be careful when we use these disciplines because, in the words of Audre Lorde, *"...the master's tools will never dismantle the master's house."*

Issues such as truth and justice in relationships cannot be taught from a European perspective. Even if these concepts do exist in European culture, their practice of them is so seriously flawed as to render them useless in any meaningful exploration of ethics and morality.

Goals and Objectives of an Afrikan Centered Rites of Passage Program

The major goal of an Afrikan Centered Rites of Passage Program is to define and make smooth the transition between childhood and adulthood. For instance, boys are often told that they are the man of the house when there is no adult male around. These boys usually have no idea what manhood is and have to adjust as they go, too often depending on their peers who also have no clue about manhood and womanhood. They, unfortunately, frequently depend on negative images in film and on TV. Also, many young girls have problems choosing a mate because the absence of adult males as models gives them nothing to compare a future mate with. The same situation can exist in the absence of an adult female in the environment.

The Afrikan American child is too frequently left to grow and develop on its own. As a result, many become uncontrollable parasites on their families as well as being terrorists in their communities. These children are usually unwanted in schools, unwanted in the workplace, and unwanted in their communities. They are hunted by law enforcement officials and are sent, in growing numbers, to "game reserves" called prisons.

We agree with Dr. Maulana Karenga and Dr. Asa Hilliard that the main problem facing our people in today's world is that of a cultural crisis. The frequently listed ills, such as teenage pregnancy, escalating violence in the community and the family, sexual aberrancies, and increasing numbers of scholastic failures (to name a few), are merely symptoms of the main problem, abandonment of our own cultural system and philosophical mores.

The keen understanding that our Afrikan Ancestors had to nature and nature's laws led to the beginning of what we now call "Rites of Passage." It was obvious to them that children were no different from other aspects of nature's laws led to the beginning of what we now call "Rites of Passage." It was obvious to them that children were no different from other aspects of nature in that they needed cultivation and direction. The direction was based on the needs of the community as well as the observed aptitudes of the child. All adults in the community were obligated to be a parent to every child. In this sense, the entire community was the extended family, and each adult shared responsibility for each child.

The second goal is preparation for responsible participation in the adult world. In Afrikan Centered Programs, it is felt that the path starts by going back to what is natural and right for us. The transformation from childhood to adulthood should not be left to chance and should be closely monitored and celebrated. Responsible and caring adults are made and not born. As Paul Hill, Jr. has stated, characteristics of maturity such as aspiration, inspiration, and motivation are passively and subliminally given to children through seemingly small and unimportant gestures such as the way that they are held, what and how they are fed, how and when they are consoled, how and when they are sung to, and what is said to them. This shaping and molding continue over the years with lessons that give images of what to value, what to ignore and what to pursue. The desired end result is the creation of an individual with all the rights and responsibilities that come with the title "adult."

Another goal of Rites of Passage Programs is developing what Dr. Wade Nobles called the competent, conscious, and confident youngster. This young person is committed to improving the quality of life for all people, especially those of Afrikan descent. This person would be a top-quality leader. Indeed, the development of servant leaders is a cornerstone in African centered Rites of Passage Programs.

The approach is simple and direct. Those who have already completed the transformation to adulthood must participate in the training and transformation of those who come after them. This transformation is part of the cyclical aspect of being that was previously mentioned. This cycle includes a transformation from the spirit world (the domain of the Ancestors), to birth, to childhood, to adulthood, to Eldership, to a return to the spirit world. The movement from one stage to the next involves the symbolic death of the old and birth of the new. It is the dual process of death and rebirth (to be "born again") into a new self that transforms the individual to physically, mentally, and spiritually express and defend the traditions of the community. These traditions should include honor, loyalty, service, cooperation, mutual respect, commitment, spirituality, collectivism, and excellence in all that is done. They should also include the courage to express these traditions.

The Rites of Passage Movement

During the late 1970s and early 1980s, the policy of the United States seemed to have a major paradigm shift that involved a direct frontal assault on Afrikan boys and men. On the surface, initially, it seemed as if everyone, all ethnic groups, wanted to "do something for Black boys." This so-called positive attention led to massive incarcerations, suspensions, and expulsions from schools, glorification of violent street gangs and a media blitz concerning the "failure" or "inability" of Black women to raise Black boys properly. The ultimate result of all of this "attention" led to the largest national construction project since the building of the interstate highway system. This national project concerned the building of jails and prisons. Economically, something had to take the place of the dying defense industry; and the housing, feeding, and controlling of Black populations, especially boys and men, became the replacement economy.

The Rites of Passage movement began in the United States as a response to the increasing problems faced by Black boys as a result of this paradigm shift. The movement was both reactive and proactive in its approach. It was reactive in that it was recognized that something had to be done to assure the survival of Afrikan people. During the paradigm shift of ethos in the United States, the Afrikan Centered movement was initially ill-prepared to provide serious programs to combat such a massive onslaught. However, because of years of reading, forming study groups, information dissemination, and community forums, the Afrikan Centered approach has demonstrated positive results in combating and counteracting the destructive trends and programs focused on Black boys.

The Rites of Passage movement has been proactive because of the philosophy that the more we do now to train our youth, the better they will be able to save themselves. They will also be prepared and willing to improve the conditions of others in the Afrikan community and save untold generations. In the words of Frederick Douglass, *"It is easier to build string children than to repair broken men."*

Since the existence of Rites of Passage Programs in America, the results have been positive for participants and trainers alike. Those people who observed the graduates of Rites of Passage programs were impressed and demanded more programs. This severely taxed the resources and energies of those individuals who were providing the programs. Fortunately, many of the graduates of these programs are starting programs of their own. These graduates are seeking advice and materials from the older and more established programs.

On the negative side is that many "quick-buck" artists offer *untried* and *bogus* programs to many desperate communities in need of services. Although many (but not all) of the people starting these programs mean well, too many of these programs are slavishly tied to aspects of European culture, European concepts, and European philosophies, which have never been truly successful in the Afrikan community.

How to Choose A Rites of Passage Program

Please be very selective as to who will provide training for your instructors. This person (or group) will also probably participate in developing your Rites of Passage program and can potentially influence your program's effectiveness and longevity. We believe strongly that Rites of passage programs should be institutionalized and stand as constant reminders of our culture's strength and viability.

Here are a few hints which could help you in your selection process:

1. Beware of new programs with no track records, especially if they openly criticize other programs and make hard-to-believe, fantastic claims about their success. True Afrikan Centered Rites of Passage Programs are cooperative and not competitive.
2. Make sure Afrikan history, philosophy, and values are part of the program.
3. The trainers should always be available to parents.
4. References should be available upon request by all trainers.
5. Check out all references.
6. Thoroughly review the goals of the program.
7. Speak with former graduates of the program.

You must remember that you are entrusting children into the care of others. When entrusting our children's care to others, extraordinary steps should be taken to ensure their safety. Concern about the context of training and the expected outcomes are also important.

Starting a Rites of Passage Program

There is much to do prior to beginning a Rites of Passage Program. An information gathering period is essential to determine whether a Rites of Passage program can alleviate perceived problems. It is also of critical importance to establish where your support lies in this effort. Listed below are several suggestions which could assist you in the start-up period. Some suggestions are:

1. *Establish the feasibility of a Rites of Passage Program within the structure, definition, mission, and limitations of your organization or group.*

   Before any group or organization commits to a Rites of Passage program, the need should be established. Commitments to the process must be obtained at the outset. Gather as much information as you can about the adults and youth within your group or organization as well as within the surrounding community. Research national and local statistics on youth, including pregnancy, "at-risk" status, effects and rates of divorce, crime, and violence, especially violence against women. Speak with parents, community leaders, school officials, and the youth in your community about some of the problems they see.

2. *Contact other concerned people within your group or organization.*

   There are, most likely, many other people within your group or organization as well as in your community who share your concern for the youth in your community. Getting them all involved early in the planning stages would help provide focus for your planned program and probably ensure their support later on.

3. *Identify Possible Trainers and Trainees.*

There should be a systematic way of identifying and selecting potential participants and facilitators (instructors). Previous positive experience with children is a definite plus for trainers. Willingness to learn new techniques and study new information are of paramount importance because Afrikan-centered Rites of Passage Programs challenge instructors to learn new and different information. Trainers should be individuals with whom anyone would entrust his/her children.

In selecting trainees, sometimes, depending on the organization or group, there is an already selected pool of young people. However, if this is not the case, one should determine the targeted age group, sex, emotional state, and educational attainment. The most successful results are obtained when young people actually want to participate in these Rites of Passage Programs. While some of the activities can be coeducational, most of the activities should be gender-specific (trainees and trainers).

There should be no more than a four-year age differential within the group. However, we feel that the ideal age groupings are ages 10-12, 13-15, and 16-17 for this program. The Rites of Passage Programs can be better tailored to maturity levels within these age groupings. This is also in keeping with Afrikan culture in which "age grades" are used in education. Members of the same age grade see themselves in a special relationship compared to others in the community.

4. *Train the trainers.*

The training process for those chosen to provide training for the youth needs to be defined. A bare minimum of 24 hours of training is necessary for trainers (preferably and ideally longer). Those who train the trainers should have at least five years of experience in running Rites of Passage Programs and should be willing to provide ongoing consultation to the group for a defined period of time. Each prospective trainer should understand that learning is a lifelong endeavor and be always willing to learn. They should complete the prescribed course of training, observe at least one program, and then participate in training youth in an actual program.

5. *Select the leader of the group.*

   There should always be a "go-to" person in the group. The "buck" would stop with this person, who would also lead all other facilitators. This choice should be based on merit (previous accomplishments, degree of concern, and work ethic) rather than position ("pecking order") or popularity. This person can make or break the program, so the choice is very important.

6. *Prepare the selected families.*

   Parents and guardians should be invited to participate at the start of the actual program and at the end. Before the program is formally started, there should be a meeting with all the parents and guardians. In this way, "informed consent" can be obtained because they will understand "the what, when, where, why, and how" of the Rites of Passage program. This involvement would also allow the parents to meet, interact with, and ask questions of the people to whom they will entrust their children.

7. *Identify your resources.*

   This includes financial as well as in-kind contributions. A realistic budget should be formulated to this end based on the design, needs, and available resources of each proposed program. There is no such thing as a model or average budget.

8. *Establish standards.*
   a. Commitment - facilitators should be prepared to see the entire process completed, from conception to graduation.
   b. Trust/Confidentiality-facilitators are frequently asked to deal with sensitive and confidential information. They must be able to establish their trustworthiness.
   c. Excellence-Minimal achievement is not sought from either the trainers or the trainees. In this program, excellence is the expectation.
   d. Code of Conduct - There must be mutual respect between the trainers and trainees. There must be rules by which the sessions will be governed.

9. *Selection of a safe and secure site.*

   The choice of a site is very important to the success of the instruction. The trainers and trainees must feel comfortable and safe in order for optimal benefit to occur. Cleanliness and minimal interruptions are a necessity.

10. *Establish times for daily meetings of trainers before and after sessions.*

    These pre-instruction and post-instruction meetings ensure that everyone is of the same accord. They are informal and short meetings. The pre-instruction meetings attempt to anticipate potential problems and unify approaches to planned topics. The post-instruction meetings help evaluate the session and enable the trainers to discuss specific issues regarding the trainees, individually and as a group. These meetings are also invaluable in helping the trainers know each other better and become more comfortable with each other, which is communicated to the trainees non-verbally.

11. *Establish a uniform to distinguish the group.*

This establishes group identity and feelings of sameness and being special. These uniforms can be as elaborate as a full Afrikan outfit or as simple as a T-shirt, cap or kufi, or item of jewelry.

12. *Establish methods of program evaluation.*

An evaluation component is of utmost importance in that it helps in obtaining financial backing, it helps in assessing the subject matter being taught, and it helps assess methods of teaching in specific situations. It helps in making decisions for the improvement of the program. An evaluation should be done in every step of the process, including the period of setting up the program.

13. *Develop forms.*

There should be application forms for the program, as well as permission forms for participation in the program, the field permission forms for the field trips, and health status forms. Finally, there should be certificates for the trainees marking their completion of the training.

Structure of a Rites of Passage Program

Although there is no maximum length of time for a Rites of Passage program, forty hours should be the absolute minimum standard. An optimal time of duration is a six-week period, although some programs can last as long as 9-12 months. Our optimal program has more than one part so that in Step Two, more specific and difficult subjects can be dealt with.

The program should be conducted at the same time and place for its duration. As in all things, there should be a beginning, middle, and end to the daily activities. The beginning can start with a prayer, a libation, and a pledge. Whatever beginning ritual is established, always begin the day in the same way. Prayer is critical in church or mosque programs and very helpful, though not essential in secular or publicly funded programs (that may bar prayer). Libations and pledges should be mandatory parts of both secular and faith-based programs.

The middle part of the daily activity is the topic to be covered. The daily activity should include an energizing game, a short didactic lecture, a video directly related to the goal, and/or a field trip. The same lesson can occur over several days based on the speed at which the trainees understand the material. Field trips should occur on separate days from the video lesson.

The last part of the day should revert to ritual. A summation of the day's activities should occur. Project Sankofa strongly suggests a Harambee Ceremony to conclude each day.

The provision of Rites of Passage programs for Afrikan American children is a growing movement. Afrikan Centered approaches are yielding the best results for our children. A new crop of positive and conscious Afrikan adults can counteract the current attacks and assaults upon our community. Our children are not worse than children of other ethnic groups! In fact, our children use alcohol and drugs less than their white peers. Our children are not more criminal than children of other groups! In fact, the law and its enforcement provide greater focus and attention to crimes most likely to occur in Black or poor communities. Our children can learn! Black mothers still do an excellent job of raising children, and Black men are still involved in saving and working with our children.

The Importance of Ritual

Rituals are formal activities that are repeated at predictably regular intervals (such as daily, weekly, monthly, etc.). The repetition reinforces the action and makes it second nature to the participant. In this way, the subliminal and subconscious messages in the ritual are easily learned and internalized.

Our Afrikan Ancestors believed strongly in the significance of ritual in our daily lives. Ritual helped define reality for them. It also explained the universe and reinforced the sacredness of human life and the relationship that should exist between humans, nature, and the universe. According to Malidoma Patrice Some' in *Ritual: Power, Healing and Community,* Swan/Raven & Company, Portland, 1993, *"Where ritual is absent, the young ones are restless or violent, there are no real elders, and the grown-ups are bewildered. The future is dim."*) The repetition of ritual was also a key to the linkage of individuals in the community. It was the glue of society.

Those who advocate the "Afrikan Way" feel that the path starts by going back to what is natural and right for us. Responsible and caring adults are made and not born. Aspiration, inspiration, and motivation are passively and subliminally given to children through such seemingly small and unimportant things as (to paraphrase Hill) the way they are held, what and how they are fed, how and when they are consoled, how and when they are sung to, and what is said to them. This shaping of our children continues over the years with lessons of what to value, what to ignore, and what to pursue. The desired end result is the creation of an individual who has been prepared to be admitted into membership in the world of adults with all the rights and responsibilities that come with the title "adult."

In most cultures, this final entrance into adulthood is marked by a "Rites of Passage" ceremony of some kind. This passage ceremony helps the new adult locate himself (or herself) within the surrounding community and within the universe. It is a rebirth or whm msw, as the ancient Afrikans in Kmt (ancient Egypt) called "repetition of the birth. It amounts to a spiritual and cultural rebirth and gives physical expression to the myths, traditions, and beliefs of that community.

The approach is simple and direct. Those who have gone through before must participate in the training and transformation of those who come after. This transformation is part of the cyclical aspect of being that was previously mentioned. This cycle includes transformations from the spirit world (the domain of the Ancestors) to birth to Childhood to Adulthood to Eldership to a return to the spirit world. The movement from one stage to the next involves the symbolic death of the old and birth of the new. It is the dual process of death and rebirth (to be "born again") into a new self that transforms the individual to physically, mentally, and spiritually express and defend the traditions of the community. These traditions should include honor, loyalty, service, cooperation, mutual respect, commitment, spirituality, collectivism, and excellence in all that is done. They should also include the courage to express these traditions.

It is the duty of "those who come before" to teach "those who come after" the essentials of the duality of life and nature. This is the essence of a Rites of Passage program. If we want to keep men and women in our midst, who have a sense of self and community, we must develop and implement approaches to this proper path.

Ritual is extremely important in Afrikan Centered Rites of Passage. Every day must begin and end in the same way. This will reinforce many of the philosophies and theories implicit and explicit in their training.

The daily ritual includes an opening ceremony consisting of a prayer, a libation to the Ancestors, and reciting the Pledge. This ritual should not vary. After the ritual, the training begins.

Although it may be decided that individuals be chosen alternately to lead prayer, it is suggested that, at least, on alternate days, a prayer or verse be recited by all the trainees in unison. Suggestions are the Lord's Prayer, the 23rd Psalm, the Beatitudes, or any other Bible verse. Some may choose to add (or substitute) reading *Selections from the Husia,* from *The Teachings of Ptahhotep*, or from *The Koran*.

The Pledge:

> My activities will be guided by my Afrikan mind, which tells me to do nothing to bring shame to myself, my family, or my community. In order to do this, I pledge:
>
> - To regard my community as part of my extended family and look upon the members of the community as my brothers and sisters.

- To accept the responsibility to protect my community from those who would do it harm.
- To respect my elders, my teachers, my parents, and those who provide positive guidance for the betterment of my life.
- To relieve the suffering in my community and to work with those who seek to make my community a better place to live.
- I pledge all this, for it is the way for a better world and a better community.

A pledge is not only a promise but is also the definition of what a Rites of Passage program endeavors to accomplish. In order to develop, set goals for, and measure the accomplishments of the program, there have to be clearly stated standards. The pledge details the standards to be accomplished. In brief, it is expected that the student will come to appreciate his or her role in helping to create healthy communities based upon an Afrikan understanding of the universe. The pledge is so critical to the program's success that we strongly advise that it be recited at the beginning of each session with the students.

The Pledge is recited while standing and using the call and response method (which is uniquely Afrikan). The leader reads and the trainees repeat what has been read. Trainees should be standing at attention or parade dress. Swaying back and forth during the reading should not be tolerated. The Pledge is critical to the program for it speaks to all issues to be accomplished in the program. The Pledge is a promise, which becomes integrated into the leader and trainees' subconscious minds.

The Libation is a statement calling upon our Afrikan Ancestors to bless the project with their presence. Afrikans believed in one great God whose intermediaries with mankind were The Ancestors. The Libation is also done in a call and response manner. The leader makes a statement, and the group responds. Many responses are used throughout Afrika in many languages. The one we most commonly use is from the Yoruba language, "Ase" (pronounced "ah-shay"), which means "amen."

The leader has a container full of water or some other liquid and then makes a statement. Then the audience responds by saying" Ase!" while the leader pours some of the liquid out. Rather than pour it on the floor, it is good to pour the water into a potted plant or into another larger container. All the trainees should get the opportunity to lead the libation, therefore, it is suggested that the lead role in the Libation be rotated daily.

A sample Libation is as follows:

Leader: To the uncreated creator, giver of all things, we pour this libation.

Audience: Ase!

Leader: We call upon our Ancestors, far and near, fathers of our fathers, mothers of our mothers, to be here with us.

Audience: Ase!

Leader: We ask them to render mercy and bear witness to the liberation and victory of our people.

Audience: Ase!

Leader: We ask those Afrikans of ancient Afrika, from Kemet, who laid the foundations of what we now call philosophy, religion, algebra, medicine, architecture, and other disciplines to be here with us. We ask Aha-Mena, Imhotep, Tiye, Nefertari,

Tutmosis III, Akhenaten, and Rameses II to be with us and share their brilliance.

Audience: Ase!

Leader: We ask those Afrikans who bravely fought against the force of tyranny and oppression to be here with us; we ask Nzinga, Yaa Asantewa, Cetewayo, and Chaka to be with us.

Audience: Ase!

Leader: We ask those Afrikans who perished during the Middle Passage and the Maafa, by their own hands and by the hands of others, to be here with us.

Audience: Ase!

Leader: We call those Afrikans who lived during the most horrific period in the history of mankind, who not only survived but thrived in the Hells of North America; we ask those Afrikans to be here with us.

Audience: Ase!

Leader: We ask those Afrikans that we have known, personally by us or by reputation, to be here with us. We will call their names.

Audience: (They will call the names of Ancestors)

Leader and Audience: Ase!

This can be changed but always remember that a Libation is said to Ancestors and not to living people.

At the close of each day's activities, trainees and trainers should hold hands and form a circle. Each time this is done, the leader should explain Harambee to the group.

The Harambee closing ceremony. Harambee is a word in the Ki-Swahili language of East Afrika, which means "Let us pull together." The phrase was first used as a method of unity upon the release of Jomo Kenyatta from prison in Kenya. Kenyatta had been imprisoned for several years for political reasons (he wanted freedom for his country from Britain). He had not committed a crime. While in prison, he had been treated harshly. Towards the end of his stay in prison, Kenyatta was elected President of Kenya. There was fear throughout the country that Kenyatta and his supporters would seek revenge for their cruel treatment while in prison.

In his first speech as president to his countrymen, Black and white, friend and enemy, he asked that all the people hearing his voice join hands. He then instructed them to shout "Harambee" three times, the third Harambee being the loudest. Even today, in Kenya, Harambee is used to settle disputes and other conflicts. Kenya is considered one of the most stable countries in the world, with a crime and murder rate much lower than in the United States.

In subsequent meetings, the Harambee Circle can be used at the end of the program day to recap or summarize the lessons learned. Each participant should be able to name one thing learned for the day which possesses some meaning for them. Once everyone has had their say, the group shouts "Harambee" three times, as previously described, with the last one being the loudest.

Suggested Reading

Akbar, Na'im (1991): *Visions For Black Men,* Winston-Derek Publishers, Inc., Nashville

Ani, Marimba (1994): *Yurungu: An African-Centered Critique of European Cultural Thought and Behavior.* Africa World Press, Trenton

Diop, Cheikh Anta Diop (1978): *The Cultural Unity of Black Africa.* Third World Press, Chicago.

Hill, Paul Jr. (1992): *Coming of Age: African American Male Rites of Passage, African American Images,* Chicago.

Hill, Paul Jr. (1995): *Back to the Future, Journal of African American Men,* 1(1): 41-62.

Majors, Richard and Janet Mancini Billson (1992): *Cool Pose: The Dilemmas of Black Manhood in America.* A Touchstone Book, Published by Simon and Schuster, NY

Mutisya, P. Masila (1996): *Demythologization and Demystification of African Initiation Rites: A Positive and Meaningful Educational Aspect Heading for Extinction, Journal of Black Studies* 27(1): 94-103

Oliver, William (1989): *Black Males and Social Problems: Prevention Through Afrocentric Socialization, Journal of Black Studies* 20 (1): 15-39, September

Wilson, Amos (1992): *Awakening the Natural Genius of Black Children,* Afrikan World InfoSystems, NY

My people are destroyed
for lack of knowledge...

Hosea 4:6, *The Bible*

PART II

THE PHILOSOPHY BEHIND THE STRUCTURAL UNITS

Unit One

"Yes, I'm Bad"

Positive Self-Concept

"You must not know the truth, if you are not free."

-Amos N. Wilson

This is a great time to be of Afrikan descent. At last, we have the means, the materials, and the information to rid ourselves of the mental slavery and social amnesia which has plagued us both in the Motherland and here in the United States for the last 300-500 years.

The beginning step in the process of healing ourselves lies in a clear understanding of a few universal principles related to being human and, more importantly, what precepts are needed for a positive self-concept. There are four symbolic features of being human. Each person, to be considered human, must be recognized by all four symbolic features to be complete. These four features are:

Land
History
Language
Culture

These four separate symbolic features are intertwined and related to providing the base of what we call self-concept. Self-concept is how we see ourselves or what we are, as compared to self-esteem, which is how we feel about what we are.

Land relates to an ancestral place of origin. This place can be real or mythological. For example, China is a real entity and has remained so for thousands of years. Whereas there are no real records of exactly where Israel was located. Israel was re-established after World War II in the former Palestine as the Jewish homeland. Regardless of where a person is born, they are immediately identified with their land base. Chinese people born in the United States are still considered Chinese, even though some may choose to hyphenate their identities, e.g., Chinese-Americans.

The only people on earth who consistently refuse to identify with their land base are United States citizens of Afrikan descent. Too many of those who refuse to accept their obvious Afrikanness seem to believe that to be Afrikan somehow diminishes their Americanness, even though a comparison of these two entities is akin to comparing an apple and a zebra. However, fortunately, the trend is moving toward acceptance of Afrikan ethnicity. As this trend by those of Afrikan descent grows, the acceptance of self also grows. The acceptance of Afrika is the beginning of the process of self-cure from the enduring remnants of slavery, especially mental slavery. Understanding the connectedness with our land of origin is a positive step toward becoming fully human.

History is the time dimension of memory. Denial of history is a serious problem within the Afrikan community. It has been recognized by the United Nations, Historical Societies of all hues, and most importantly, the Association for the Study of Classical Afrikan Civilizations (ASCAC) that the reestablishment of Afrikan history is essential to the growth and development of, not only Afrikan people, but also, world civilization. But you ask, how important is history? Let us look briefly at a study done by Bernard Aaronson and published by Omni magazine in February 1984, called "Timeless Mind."

In the study, college students were hypnotized and given a post-hypnotic suggestion, which simply stated, "when you awaken the past will be gone." When the college students were awakened, they were described as drowsy and infantile, having lost both memory and the ability to speak. Next, the students were told, again under hypnosis, that they had no future. When awakened, these students had lost all sense of identity and motivation and had become euphoric.

The study went on further to cancel the present in the minds of the students. Students exhibited signs of depression and schizophrenic behavior. The students later described the total experience as "living death." As described in this study, history is the essential ingredient involved in human growth and development and, indeed, sanity.

Afrikan philosophy maintains that there is no division between the past, the present, and the future. The study, as mentioned above, proves this philosophy to be correct. It is impossible for a well-functioning human to continue to be well functioning without a total sense of history. We learn from this study that history can be manipulated. Those in charge of the manipulation can control sanity and reality. In the end, the correct and truthful teaching of verifiable history is essential for assuming positive human roles and concepts.

Much of the recent historical discoveries have been jokingly criticized as "feel good history." We maintain that history has been a tool for feeling good about oneself for a long time. The difference now is that accurate history is being used to create feelings of positive self-concept and self-esteem for people of Afrikan origin. "Feel good history" is not all bad as long as it is truthful and accurate.

The combination of land and history in this context demonstrates to the student that they are an integral and very important part of a very long process that started long before the low point in which we did not find ourselves. They need to realize that their people knew greatness thousands of years ago and that they are not only capable of continuing that greatness but are expected to do so.

Language is the symbolic means of conveying and sharing culture. A substantial number of Afrikans speak several languages. In the United States, most Afrikans speak a form of Anglicized Bantu tongue (Ebonics) and/or Americanized English. Neither American English nor Ebonics is truly English. Both are separate language groups.

The symbolic effects of a language convey what is important in a culture. There is only one word for "love" in the English language. Yet there are several words that describe "war" such as riot, insurgency, insurrection, rebellion, conflict, guerilla action, battler, strife, belligerency, and hostilities. This might suggest that "love" is less important than war in English.

In many Afrikan languages, there are no words for aunt, uncle or cousin. There is only mother, father, brother, and sister. All elders considered all children as sons and daughters. Elders are treated as mother and father. Everyone in the same age group was considered to be brothers and sisters. Linguistically, this tradition is carried on in most Black Churches, regardless of denomination. The terms brother and sister are used frequently in our religious contexts and in our social/community interactions.

Connecting to language is important and being multilingual in the present is extremely important. Afrikan language forms are of equal importance and just as correct as any other form of language. Language, though, has a power context. At one time, French was felt to be the most important language internationally, but this is no longer true. A few years ago, there was a great rush to learn Chinese. Those wishing to trade in Afrika have to learn to read, write, and speak Ki-Swahili, which is the trade language of the Eastern, Central, and Southern regions of Afrika. Language is the conveyor of social relationships, including economic relationships. Humans relate in both social and economic terms. To be fully human is to be able to use and recognize language for its true purposes.

Though considered a separate heading, culture is, in truth, the binder of Land, Language, and History. Culture translates symbols into reality and behavior. Culture gives life to philosophy and provides the basis for understanding self and others. How often have you heard, "I wonder what makes Black people act like that?

In this context, cultural deprivation becomes clear. Black people act less than human when means of adhering to those humanizing factors are denied, hidden, or stolen from us. However, if memory is restored by connectedness and cultural competence, then people of Afrikan descent can grow, develop, prosper and flourish.

Once the basics are understood or, at least, some understanding and acceptance of the concepts concerning land, language, culture, and history, then a person or group can operationalize the cornerstones of self-concept.

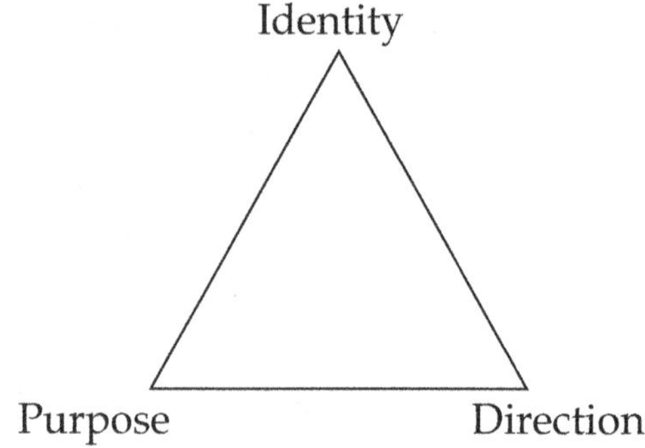

Those cornerstones and Identity, Purpose, and Direction. Just as a person must have land, language, culture, and history to be human, each human has tasks to accomplish in the present and future, using the past as the base.

Identity

The task of identity is to determine who you are. Of course, this task is not difficult if your identity (who you are) is not under attack. Afrikans have gone through many transitional name changes. Our ancestors began as kinship group names such as Mandinka, Ashanti, Fulani, Zulu, Igbo, Hausa, Yoruba, and many others. Our knowledge of our kinship groups was largely destroyed during the Maafa (great disaster) of the past five hundred years. Our identity then is tied to the entire continent of Afrika. This is important in that the degree of mental enslavement is best diagnosed by those who protest the loudest against connectedness to Afrika. No other group of human beings on earth protests so loudly and foolishly against the very foundation of their humanity.

You would never hear an Irishman, Japanese, Italian, German, or Norwegian, though born in the United States, deny their connection to Ireland, Japan, Italy, Germany, or Norway. Yet there are "Negroes" who cling to the idea that others should name us, tell us our identity, tell us where we come from, and with what we can and cannot be connected. A Negro can never be truly free because denial of reality and truth is so great as to render the person a perpetual slave. The very acts of identifying oneself, naming oneself, and living according to that identity and name define how the world views you. It is not a matter of like or dislike. It is a matter of self-respect or disrespect of self. Negroes are most concerned that the "master" likes them, while Afrikans demand respect. Which is most important?

You are viewed as free or controlled, sane or insane, knowing or unknowing based on how you understand yourself. Interestingly, if you cannot understand self, then it is presumed that you cannot understand others. However, once a person understands self by developing a collective identity, new questions arise concerning existence.

Purpose

The question of existence is concerned with answering, "Why am I here? What purpose is there for my being here, at this time, and in this place?" Again, being grounded is important. We are products of and indebted to the past. Understanding the debt owed to the past and, ironically, the future determines our purpose. Our purpose is truly our daily struggle toward some goal or contribution toward civilizing the world. Another question arises, "What part of the human struggle do I take as my personal responsibility? What has been completed by the Ancestors, and what have they left for me to accomplish?" These are life-long and continuous questions which can be answered at each stage of life. The answers of children would be different from the answers of adults and elders. Once there is clarity as to one's purpose, then the next task is to answer the question of how to achieve that purpose.

Direction

The answer to the question of achieving purpose is called the task of direction. If I know who I am and why I am here, then accomplishing the whys for living becomes the task. The accomplishment of reaching multiple purposes tends to provide for a continual transformation of identity. This continual transformation is called growth. One definition of growth is the accumulation of knowledge. As a person accumulates more knowledge, they, in turn, put that knowledge to practical use. The use of knowledge is wisdom. Wisdom, then, can also be considered growth.

Those who stop learning, accumulating, and using knowledge are, in fact, dead. They may still be breathing, but for all intents and purposes, they have mentally and spiritually died. Direction modifies and adds to identity. The lack of direction in one's life leads to deterioration and death, and decomposition.

The Christian Bible states clearly that you shall know the truth and that truth shall make you free. Are you free to know the truth? Are you free to connect to Afrika, or is something holding you back from such connectedness? In reality, you are connected to your people whether you want that connection or not. Are you free to learn about those things which make you human? Being human is not a birthright. It is a mental concept of acceptance of self and acceptance of those who have similar identities to self. If you cannot be who you truly are because someone else makes that choice for you, then you cannot be free.

If someone other than you is in control of your past, present, and future, then you are not free. If you cannot name yourself because someone else is offended by that name, you are not free. If you cannot base your decisions upon reality and truth, then you are not free. If you cannot work in the best interest of your identified kinship group, as can be done by all ethnic and racial groups, without being made to feel guilty, then you are not free.

Though these truisms are not easy to refute, they are hard to accept by many self-deluded people of Afrikan descent. If you are self-determining and that self-determination is based upon truth and reality, then you are truly free and truly human. For people of Afrikan descent, reality can only be based upon a connectedness to Afrika. The truth shall make you free.

As Ausa people, we must also connect to those Ausa heroes and sheroes who have consistently demonstrated a dedication to excellence along with a conscious connection to Afrika. This would include individuals such as Malcolm X, Marimba Ani, Martin Luther King, Jr., Fannie Lou Hamer, Martin Delany, Ida B. Wells Barnett, W.E.B. DuBois, David Walker, and Maya Angelou (among many others).

In developing a Rites of Passage program, it is essential that positive self-concept be worked on with the trainees (and trainers) first. It is the prerequisite to all other learning. The control of self, which is known as discipline, is essential if the trainee is to benefit from further teachings. Positive self-concept may consume several meetings to accomplish. The older the youth or young adults involved, the longer the process.

If the potential trainers have never been exposed to Afrikan Centered thought and philosophy, it may be harder for them to grasp the concepts. The depth of the "brainwashing" of Afrikan children begins before reaching school age and then continues in pre-school, and by the sixth grade, many of the negative stereotypes have been so implanted into their psyches as to render it very difficult for the child to achieve excellence. Potential trainers have been subjected to this "brainwashing" also and have to be "de-programmed" through training. It is essential that trainers in Rites of Passage programs be trained and commit themselves to continuous learning once the initial training is complete.

SUGGESTED EXERCISES ON POSITIVE SELF CONCEPT

Self-concept is the catchall term used by social scientists to describe a combination of self-esteem, identity, direction and purpose. We all have a self-concept, and it tells the world who we are and with what we are concerned.

The ROP Program deals with developing a positive self-concept through a series of exercises, lectures, field trips and videos. The issues involved in developing a positive self-concept are critical to the success of working with our youth.

Materials needed: Flip chart and markers
PowerPoints
television and VCR
transportation for the field trip

Didactic portion: Short lecture (15 minutes) defining and discussing Identity, Purpose, and Direction.

Experiential portion: Identity game
What is a man/woman exercise?

Video: "Roots" (first installment only)

Field trip: Outline prominent Black historical persons and places in your city. (AME churches and Masonic lodges. Give an excellent intro into discussions of famous persons outlined below). Include also Black banks, black-owned business (past and present) and other places of interest.

Biography (see Glossary): George Washington Carver
Martin Luther King, Jr
Anna Julia Cooper
Richard Allen
Prince Hall
Maria Stewart

Literature: *On the Origin of Things* by Listervelt Middleton. This poem must be thoroughly read, analyzed, and studied in minute detail. It will teach history as well as drive an understanding of historical concepts.

Expected Outcomes

Upon completion of this exercise:

a) Participants will be able to define and explain Identity, Purpose, and Direction.
b) Participants will be able to relate the concepts of Identity, Purpose, and Direction to the lives of the historical figures named, as well to their own lives.
c) Participants will be able to understand the concept of humanity and the four basic concepts of being human.
d) Participants will be able to recognize and appreciate good men (and women) in order to hopefully model their lives after positivity.

e) Participants will be able to recognize and appreciate their roles and responsibilities as members of the Ausa People.

Didactic

Prior to beginning any unit, there must be preplanned ***short*** lectures (no longer than ten minutes), which set the stage for the learning process. At the beginning of each unit, information is given which will assist in developing the short lecture. These didactic lectures provide focus for the learning that follows using the other outlined techniques.

The lecture for this unit, "A Reconnection with Afrika," is essential for the growth and development of trainees (The preparation will help the trainers, also). The American models of culture have not worked in sufficient numbers to assist the majority of our people. For our people and for any people, it is necessary to accomplish three philosophical tasks in a lifetime (which were originally posed by Dr. Franz Fanon). The first task is to determine who you are. This is the task of identity. All Americans are immigrants. All other immigrants have a basic universal identity. Because of colonization and enslavement, continental Afrikans and Diasporic Afrikans lack their true identities. This restructuring of an Afrikan identity becomes the first task of a Rites of Passage program. We feel that the only difference between colonization and enslavement is location and, in some instances, methodology.

The second task is to determine, "Are you really who you think you are?" Afrikans who live in America are called by many names. What is really our name? Who gave us these names? What do these names mean? How does a name affect how we see ourselves? How does a name affect how we behave and what we can accomplish?

The last life task is to ask ourselves, "Are we all that we can be?" A label can be a limit. Sometimes the names and definitions attached to those names can limit us in our achievement.

The cornerstones, then, to human life are to determine IDENTITY, PURPOSE, AND DIRECTION. To accomplish becoming fully human, one has to have a positive identity, purpose, and direction. However, being human is not a birthright. To be identified as human, there are four qualifiers. You have to have a land named after you, a history written about you by you, a language you can call your own, and a culture that is all yours.

In brief, to be human, you must have land, language, culture, and history as a prerequisite. To accomplish your life tasks, you must have identity, purpose, and direction.

Experiential

Each unit uses the experiential lessons to reinforce the lecture. During the didactic phase, trainees sit and listen passively. During the experiential sessions, trainees are actively involved in mental and physical exercises, which test the validity of the lecture in the didactic sessions.

During the lecture, a flip chart should be used to illustrate the key points. When talking about identity, purpose, and direction, the following diagram should be drawn.

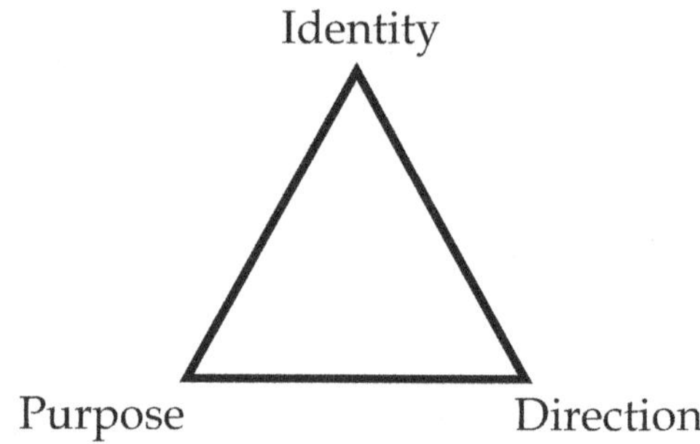

Also, these words should be listed on the chart on another page: **Land, Language**, **Culture**, and **History**. These four words denote the four qualifiers for being considered human.

Exercise #1 The Identity Game

To get the trainees on task, ask a series of questions:

- If a man entered the room and looked Asian, where do you think he originally came from?
- If the same man spoke and you did not understand the language, what type of language would you presume that he was speaking?
- If the same man went home and read a history book about his people, what history would he be reading?
- If, after he finished reading, he got up to eat, what type of food would he eat?

After answering the questions aloud, the trainees are divided into the following groups and given this task. With the names you assign to each group, they determine if their group can be fully human. Each group is given one name, and they are as follows: **Negro, Colored, Black, African American, and Afrikan.**

Each group determines whether their group name has a land, language, culture, and history by answering Yes or No. A spokesman should be chosen from each group (he or she may continuously communicate with their groups). If the answer is No, go on. If there is a Yes answer, ask the group to explain. If there is confusion, the answer is No. The final answer is that no group other than "Afrikan" meets the criteria for being fully human. Thus those who accept the other names are treated as less than human. Carefully review the lecture in the didactic session. An easy way to visually handle this exercise is to use the flip chart and develop the following graph.

NAME	LAND	LANGUAGE	CULTURE	HISTORY
Negro				
Colored				
Black				
African American				
Afrikan				

This exercise could take 30 to 60 minutes to complete depending upon the amount of discussion. Be prepared for surprise answers, confusion, and heated debates. If you remember how easy it was to describe a Chinese as a human, you can keep a group focused. There should be no confusion about a person's humanity. Names other than Afrikan cause confusion. A Chinese person is Chinese no matter where he is born, the language he speaks, the clothes he wears, or the length of time in another country. This is true of all people except when dealing with Blacks, Afro Americans, etc. To fully join the human race, we must accept our Afrikan heritage as the totality of our essence.

The second exercise in this unit deals with the definition of self. Our children are bombarded with negative messages daily. The degree to which these negative messages occur is largely undocumented. In the exercise entitled **What is a Man/Woman**, you will need to be prepared to hear words and expressions that our children hear daily. You will not like what you hear but list these words anyway. This exercise builds trust between the trainers and trainees and will have positive results later in the program. Stress to them that they may communicate freely (within bounds of decency).

Exercise #2 What is a Man/Woman?

Using a flip chart, have the trainees provide you with information on the following questions:

"Tell me the bad or negative things that you have heard said about Black men?" Repeat the question for women.

List their responses on the flip chart. Label the page negative. In most instances, you will have to call a halt because the negatives that children hear could take up all of the pages on your flip chart. When you fill one page, stop. Tape their responses to the wall in a noticeable place.

The second question is as follows: "What are the characteristics of a good man/woman?" Again, list their responses, label this list positive, and find a conspicuous place to display them.

The third question is key. "Which list do you want to be on?" Most children will want to be on the positive list. Go back to the lecture diagram of identity, purpose and direction. Lead a discussion using the negative and positive lists. Encourage their feedback.

This exercise is an excellent way of introducing a discussion of male/female relationships and covering issues of respect for the "complementary" sex. Explain why males and females are "complementary" rather than "opposite."

Media

Roots (Volume I only)

The popular film Roots is easy to obtain from either a local video store or the public library. There are several volumes, but you will only need the first volume. The story begins in Afrika and ends on a slave ship bound for the Americas. The videos support didactic and experiential learning. This method appeals to our children because of their addiction to television.

For this reason, the videos were selected because they show Afrikan people in a positive light and overcoming struggles that have relevance today. These videos are not to be viewed for entertainment but as learning tools that reinforce the unit information being learned. The technique for viewing videos is to:

a) First, pass out a set of questions to the trainees.
b) After they have read the questions, have them place the questions under their chairs.
c) Start the film and stop it every half hour.

At these breaks, discuss the questions. Before showing any film, make sure that all trainers have seen the film, know where to break the film, and are familiar with the questions. The questions for ROOTS are listed below.

ROOTS QUESTIONS 1

1. What year was Kunta Kinte born in West Africa?
2. What was important about the child's name?
3. When Kunta was guarding his father's goats, what kind of animal did he scare away?
4. What did his father think about Kunta scaring away the animal and what advice did he give?

The key elements of these questions and this part of the video reveal family life in Afrika. Two principles to be taught and talked about are that all people make mistakes and that we should learn from them (so as not to repeat them). The second principle deals with removing oneself from danger. Never run toward dangerous animals or situations. Ask trainees what they do when they hear a gunshot in their neighborhood or if they see someone fighting at school. Compare and discuss their answers in relation to the father's advice in the video.

ROOTS QUESTIONS 2

1. What did they call the man in charge of the Manhood Training?
2. What was his advice to the boys?
3. How do you learn according to the man in charge?
4. What kind of courage does the warthog have?
5. What was Kunta Kinte's mission? Why did he not complete his mission?
6. What was the wise man of the village's advice to the boys in Manhood Training (about what Kunta saw)?

This portion of the video addresses the issue of Rites of Passage in Afrika. This experience is similar to that which they are going through, except this is a modern version. Notice that the boys in the video are subject to lessons from elders.

ROOTS QUESTIONS 3

1. What present did Kunta's father give him?
2. What did his mother give him?
3. What was the first rule that Kunta Kinte broke?
4. What other rules did Kunta break?
5. What was the Passage that the sailor talked about?
6. What were Kunta's escape plans?

This section of the video deals with the difference between knowledge and wisdom. Elders taught methods of staying out of trouble, yet Kunta disregarded this knowledge and lost his freedom. Knowledge is a collection of facts based on present and past reality, but wisdom is the ability to use knowledge appropriately in all situations. Wisdom can only be attained through life experiences and time. Kunta broke every rule, including disrespecting an elder (his mother), not using his senses by going out alone, traveling through tall bushes, and not heeding the smell of wet chickens. "The Passage" speaks to the trip between Afrika and the Americas called the Middle Passage.

ROOTS QUESTIONS 4

1. What did the white man mean when he said, "There goes 100 guineas to the sharks"?
2. What was Kunta's dream about?

3. What plan did the Wrestler tell Kunta on how to defeat the white man?
4. Why couldn't all of the Afrikans on the ship understand one another?

This portion deals with the Middle Passage. Trainees need to know that their ancestors (great-great grandparents) were brought here as part of the slave trade where Afrikan people were bought and sold like pigs, horses, and cows. They were forced to work for free after being kidnapped from their families in Afrika. One method of keeping down revolts on slave ships was to put Afrikans on board who spoke different languages. Wrestler's plans hoped to overcome this obstacle. Slave narratives (found in the public library) tell of nightmares concerning Afrikans being in the belly of white beasts.

Field Trip

Field trips are essential parts of the program. A Black History tour of your area is a good way to show trainees that our people are remembered through buildings, streets, schools, churches, mosques, and parks named after them. Regardless of the size of the town or city, there are many Black Historic sites in your area. This usually takes a little research or asking elders about sites of importance.

References and Suggested Reading for Unit One

Adams, Russell L. *Great Negroes: Past and Present.* Chicago: Afro-Am Publishing Company, 1984

Akbar, Na'im. *Visions for Black Men.* Nashville: Winston-Derek Publishers, Inc., 1991

Fanon, Franz. *Black Skins, White Masks*. NY: Grove Press, 2008

Hilliard, Asa G. *The Maroon Within Us: Selected Essays on African American Community Socialization*, Baltimore: Black Classic Press, 1995

Hilliard, Asa G. *SBA: The Reawakening of the African Mind*. Gainesville, FL: Makare Publishing Company, 1997

Kambon, Kobi Kazembe Kalomgi. *The African Personality in America: An African-Centered Framework*, Tallahassee: Nubian Nation Publications, 1992

Kuykendall, Crystal. *From Rage to Hope: Strategies for Reclaiming Black and Hispanic Students*, Bloomington: National Educational Service, 1992

Welsing, Frances Cress. *The Isis Papers: The Keys to the Colors*. Lawrenceville, NJAfrica World Press, 2004

Wilson, Amos N. *The Developmental Psychology of the Black Child*, NY: African Research Publications, 1978

Unit Two
"Not that Black Stuff Again"

African History, Philosophy, and Culture

"The present is...lost if we forget our past and have no vision of the future."

- Ayi Kwei Armah, *The Healers*

In Afrikan culture, the observation of nature shaped human behavior. The people understood the cyclical nature of life and how all things in nature benefited all other things. There was a sense of purpose and order. Survival of all depended upon the preservation of this cyclical relationship.

The forces of nature also shaped the European world. The millennia spent in the hostile environment of the Wurm interglacial (Ice Age) taught him the principle of "Survival of the fittest" (strongest). The European male, as the strongest, began to understand survival as a phenomenon of the individual. He understood that in that reality, the idea of a strong individual ("rugged individualism") was of more immediate importance than the need for a strong community. Women and female children were viewed as weak possessions and a potential source of man's weakness. Only the strong were meant to survive. Kinship networks were scattered because the necessities of life were scarce, and there was not enough to go around. The idea of sharing was seen as a foolish, sentimental, and potentially fatal mistake. The extended family in the Afrikan sense did not/could not exist in Europe. Death, destruction, and domination were the traits that would become a very important part of the spirit of survival. Deceit and cunning were admired methods of achieving the "three Ds." These traits are now manifested by both men and women in Western culture.

The basic mindset that was started in the ice has dictated much of the course of the last five hundred years of our existence. Even in the less hostile temperate environment of the United States, individual cunning and deceit are prized above community. Many of the most popular films, books, and television programs elevate the notion of the individualistic loner who is "appropriately" violent and who uses everything and everyone around him in order to achieve his goals. Even criminals are frequently portrayed in a sympathetic light and turned into tragic folk heroes, such as Bonnie and Clyde, the Italian Mafia in "The Godfather" films, and Butch Cassidy and the Sundance Kid. Misguided efforts by white women and Men of Afrikan Origin (and some Women of Afrikan Origin) have produced some programs/films in which a woman performs the violent, cunning acts. Unfortunately, this is viewed as "progress."

In real life, it is all right to exploit and literally cheat others in the name of "profit" as long as the "rules" are not broken, such as Worldcom, Wallstreet, subprime lenders, and payday lenders. Even those who break the rules are called names like "embezzlers" and are not considered to be common thieves. Frequently, the greater the value of the object stolen, the less harsh the penalty if caught. This is survival of the strongest at its very best.

This mindset, this "cult of individuality," has invaded the Afrikan community and is now pervasive. It has translated itself into a siege of our communities in which we are our own captives. We fear ourselves and our children. This dangerous situation has to be corrected, and the philosophy of individualism must be rejected.

In order for our youth to reject the "cult of individuality," an alternative must be presented. The alternative must help the individual see himself/herself as part of a cultural collective. In the Afrikan centered program *Project: Sankofa,* history is taught from several aspects. In this program, the purpose is to help our youth understand that they are part of a cultural collective through the teaching of history.

Before moving forward to actual events in history, there are three very important questions that must be answered. The first question is, "What is the role of history?" The preeminent scholar and historian, the late Dr. John Henrik Clarke, professor emeritus at Hunter College in New York City, has said in many of his lectures: *"History is a clock people use to tell their political time of day. It is also a compass that people use to find themselves on the map of human geography. History tells a people where they have been and what they have been. It tells a people where they are and what they are. Most importantly, history tells a people where they still must go and what they still must be."*

The role of history is not just to tell about the past (Identity) but also to inform us as Afrikan people about our purpose in life, which is, in great part, to understand and pay our debt to our past.

The next question that should be discussed is, "What is history?" Maulana Karenga has defined history in this way, *"History is the struggle and record of humans in the process of humanizing the world, i.e., shaping it in their own image and interests. To shape the world in a human image is to give it a human form and character and to shape it in human image is to give it a human form and character and to shape it in human interests is to make it serve humans rather than threaten, deform or destroy them."*

If this is true, then Afrikan history is the struggle and record of Afrikans in the process of Afrikanizing the world, i.e., shaping it in their own image and interests. Defining history is very important because it gives clear direction as to how history can fit into everyday life.

The third and final question is, "What are some of the characteristics of history?" History is a process in which you find human beings in definite social situations in relation to themselves, to others, and to nature. As was stated earlier, history is a series of struggles. These struggles, being fully human, will be full of conflict and contradictions. The characteristics of conflict and contradiction must be seen against four major opponents, nature, society, others, and self. By not just focusing on the achievements of Afrikan people but also on the conflicts and struggles they endured, the trainee/student will understand that problems can be resolved in ways other than violently. Death, destruction, and domination are not the only way people resolve their problems.

Now that the role, definition, and characteristics of history have been discussed, a chronological order to the telling of our story must be given to help in developing a broader view of history. Afrikans in America have been hiding behind the veil of slavery for too long. This veil of slavery must be removed so Afrikans can see what they accomplished in the building of independent states.

In order to accomplish this, we must start by using a list based on the different eras in the history of Afrikan people. Below is a suggested chronological list:

1. Early man (recognition of first humans, especially the Twa people and culture).
2. Predynastic North Afrika and Ancient Kemet (Egypt) (recognition of first civilization).
3. Empires of East Afrika (Axum, Kush, Kerma, Punt).
4. Empires of the Western Sudan (Ghana, Mali, Songhay, the Hausa States, Benin, Kanem-Bornu, etc.).
5. Moors in Spain (seven hundred years of development) (including Arabic slave trading).
6. European Slave Trade.
7. Afrikan Liberation Movements and Slave Revolts in the Caribbean, Brazil, and the U.S.

8. Pan-Afrikan Nationalism in the U.S. and the Caribbean.
9. The Civil War and Reconstruction.
10. The Post-Reconstruction era.
11. The Harlem Renaissance era.
12. The Newly Independent Afrikan countries.
13. The Civil Rights era and the Post Civil Rights era.
14. The Rebirth of Pan-Afrikan Nationalism.

The above topics are only a basic outline. There are more specific outlines and curriculums available (see bibliography at the end of this book). It is also strongly suggested that a timeline be used in order to understand the true chronological flow of history.

The history of Afrikan people must start with early man, and then it must proceed to the first four Golden Ages of Afrika, which occurred in Kemet (Ancient Egypt). Our definition of a golden age is when social, political, and economic development and expansion is actively and creatively occurring. Ancient Kemet had the good fortune of having more than 3,000 years of uninterrupted cultural development and expansion, from 3100 B.C.E. to 332 B.C.E.

No other group of people in the history of the world has had the kind of development and expansion that these ancient Afrikans experienced. The first buildings of stone (Pyramids and Temples) were erected by indigenous Afrikan people. In order to erect buildings of stone, one had to have a theoretical and practical knowledge of mathematics. The art of surgery was quite advanced in Ancient Kemet. The Kamieu wrote medical textbooks, such as the "Ebers" Papyrus (a medical textbook) and the "Edwin Smith" Papyrus (a surgical textbook). In 1650 B.C.E., the Kemetic scribe, Ahmose, wrote formulas for the area of a triangle. It was in ancient Kemet that the first calendar was designed (in order to design and use a calendar, one has to know and understand seasonal changes, mathematics, astronomy, and astrology).

The fifth Golden Age of Afrika involved the great West and Southern Afrikan empires of Ghana, Mali, Songhay, Great Zimbabwe, the Zulu Empire, Kanum Bornu as well as the Hausa States and other prominent and advanced groups. The first three empires named lasted approximately 1,200 years, starting around 350 A.C.E. with the rise of probably one of its greatest kings, Tenkamenin. Ghana was known for its gold which attracted people from other parts of the world. Ghana also became known throughout the world for its political organization and social formation. People came from all over the world to study at the University of Sankore in Timbuktu.

No story of the great west Afrikan empires can be complete without mentioning the great king of Mali, Mansa Musa. He was one of the most colorful Afrikan Kings of the fourteenth century. Mali under King Mansa Musa was known for its great architecture and for the honesty of the people. The king himself was known for his regal splendor and is known as being the wealthiest man that the world has ever known. Europe during this time in history was still in its medieval period.

The Songhay King that history has recorded as one of Afrika's most powerful Heads of State was Askia the Great. It has been said that his realm was larger than all of Europe. Askia came to power in 1493, a year after Columbus left for the new world. His reign lasted until his death in 1528 A.C.E. Songhay was never able to recapture the glory it knew under Askia the Great.

The light that had shone so brightly in Afrika was beginning to dim. Afrika, which had contributed so much to the world by way of social and family formation, which had taught the world what democracy and constitutional law ought to be about, had now reached a period in its long history that would forever change the course of human history. The European "slave trade" was one of the most devastating and destructive periods in world history.

One compelling reason to use a chronological list is that it allows one to put slavery in its proper perspective. The European enslavement of Afrikan people was just one of the periods in our long history. It was, however, a very important period in the sense of its devastating effect on Afrikan people left on the continent, as well as on the ones who were taken away. The imperialistic imperative and cultural aggression displayed by European and Arab people in the Motherland and her descendants in America has been the greatest crime ever committed against humanity. These effects are still prevalent in the way Afrikans feel about themselves today. Dr. Marimba Ani, in her book, *Let the Circle Be Unbroken,* called this period in history "The Maafa," which is a Ki-Swahili term for "Great Disaster."

In the teaching and telling of the Maafa, one should always consider what preceded it. What precipitated the Maafa? How was it carried out? Who were the players involved? Who were some of the heroes/sheroes that the history books in most public educational institutions failed to mention or only mentioned in passing? The names read like a Who's Who list, Harriet Tubman, Denmark Vesey, Sojourner Truth, David Walker, Henry Highland Garnet, Hosea Easton, Maria Stewart, Martin R. Delany, and many more who were left off the pages of history in the public school textbooks.

A chronological list should cover the reawakening of the Afrikan spirit of liberation and nationalism. When did this spirit of liberation start, and who were some of the people involved? When did the spirit of Afrikan nationalism start in America? Is that same spirit alive and well today? If so, then who are some of the modern-day people involved in this struggle?

The selections on the above chronological list are arbitrary, but it is felt by the authors that these are the most essential eras in the history of Afrikan people. We, as Afrikan people, must be at the forefront when it comes to the telling of our history. It cannot be left in the hands of others. The ramifications are too heavy a price to pay.

Napoleon Bonaparte once said, *"What is history but a fiction agreed upon?"* We can interpret this to mean that history is something to be controlled and manipulated, especially the writing and telling of it. If one has the control and power over the writing and telling of not just their history but of your history also, then they control what and who you are as a people.

Dr. Wade Nobles, retired Black Studies Professor at San Francisco State University, defines power this way: *"Power is the ability to define reality and have others respond to your definition as if it were their own."*

The manipulation and distortion of history and especially Afrikan history, has contributed greatly to the low self-esteem and the "Cult of Individualism" that is prevalent in the Afrikan American community. When a people don't know who and what they are, then they become, as our noted historian Dr. Carter G. Woodson once said, *"A negligible factor in the thought of the world."*

This can be blatantly seen when there is a "G7" meeting where the world's most powerful men representing the seven most powerful nations in the world get together, and not one Afrikan man or nation is represented. This seems even more profoundly ironic when one considers that the riches that have made the countries represented by the "G7" powerful came from Afrika (directly or indirectly). When the history of Afrikans is taught in the public school systems in this country, it always begins with slavery. The impression that is given early in a child's development is that their people can never rise above working for or being in service to Europeans.

As Daniel Patrick Moynihan, the esteemed Senator from the state of New York, and Nathan Glazer, a noted historian and member of the New York state board of regents, which oversees the curriculum and policies for all public schools in the state of New York, wrote in their celebrated book, *Beyond the Melting Pot, "The Negro is only an American and nothing else. He has no values and culture to respect or protect."*

It is within this context that Afrikans find themselves having to be defenders of their history and culture. Afrikans are the most written about people in the history of the world. The onslaught of disinformation being disseminated about Afrikan people makes one wonder why those who claim to be superior spend so much time writing about Afrikan inferiority. Could it be that those who claim to be superior understand that if Afrikan people ever knew the truth about their history and culture, their position in the world as the power brokers may cease to exist? Dr. John Henrik Clarke has repeatedly said that *"you can't oppress a historically conscious people."* To paraphrase Dr. John Henrik Clarke, if we begin our history with slavery, everything that happens afterwards seems like an improvement.

Today's youth must be able to identify and define the appropriate time periods in the history of Afrikan people in which we struggled. They must also see that struggle is a problem that can and must be solved. If they ask the right questions, they will solve the problem and end the struggle. Too many of our youth do not see the validity in learning or studying our history because Afrikan and Afrikan American history is usually told as a boring series of dates and biographical sketches. History can be fascinating and transformative when it is taught as a way to answer questions that solve problems. In order for history to be transformative, our youth must see themselves in the telling of it. They must be involved in the studying of our history, and problem-solving situations must be presented to fully understand the struggle of their Ancestors.

In *Project Sankofa, A Rites of Passage Program,* it is our aim to produce the kind of young men and women who will "Honor" their Ancestors, remain "Loyal" to their culture, and be of "Service" to Afrikan people.

History plays a profoundly prominent role in the practice of Sankofa.

Suggested Exercises on Afrikan History, Philosophy, and Culture

A people's ideology, worldview, and behaviors are shaped by its response to experiences encountered through time. This unit provides participants with an understanding of the nature of History, the principles of Traditional African Philosophy, and the meaning of Culture.

The painfully repressed collective memories of enslavement are revisited to learn lessons that will be useful for future use of a positive self-concept.

Materials: Same as previously

Didactic: Ask questions and discuss the answers:

1) What is history?
2) What lessons can be learned from history? (An example of trying to avoid a bully who's beaten you or someone you know can be given as "learning from history").
3) How can history build character?
4) How can history be used negatively?
5) Discuss timelines of History using general division into pre-Maafa, Maafa, and post-Maafa.

Experiential: Matching game:

Video: ***Sankofa***

Biography: (See Glossary) Imhotep
Martin Delany
Hatshepsut
Makeda
Frances Cress Welsing
Franz Fanon
Chinweizu

Literature: *The Negro Speaks of Rivers* by Langston Hughes (Analyze each verse.) What do you think the writer was trying to say?

Field Trip: Any Afrikan-oriented museum or business that can speak about or show African artifacts or artifacts from the past.

Expected Outcomes: This Unit is a continuation of Unit One. Upon completion of this Unit, the trainee should have concretized the **Identity** concept. He/she should also have begun to think about **Purpose** in a less abstract way.

Didactic

In a lecture on the history of Afrikan people, use as many visual aids as necessary. Flip charts or PowerPoint presentations will be necessary. It is important to start in ancient, pre-colonial Afrika and then proceed to the Americas. Stress that we had several thousands of years of history prior to the Arab and European invasion and the enslavement of Afrikan people. Timelines can put the issue of history visually into perspective for trainees because the general public is usually unaware of time frames of history. A picture is worth a thousand words and use transparencies whenever possible. The timeline developed by Anthony Browder will be especially helpful. Also, brush up on Kemetic and other Afrikan history in the references provided. Guest lecturers may also be appropriate at this time, but it is better that the trainers are able to give the trainees this information.

The historical information should be carefully considered and presented so as to relate the past to the present. Dry lectures with frequent use of dates without dealing with "the why's" WILL definitely turn most young people off. There has to be purpose in each bit of information given. In order for one to be able to use history to frame the future, it must be made relevant to the present. There are many (some painful) lessons to be learned from the study of our past. It is critically important that we learn them.

An overview of our history must be included in any ROPP and must start at the beginning. This discussion must also include a political analysis of pertinent historical occurrences from the perspective of the trainees (individually and as a group).

A brief discussion of how history has been used against us will also be of interest and importance. Please take care to avoid letting this part turn into a biographical listing. Any mention of a person should include not only what he/she did but should also include the significance of what they gave to the world, then and today, and should be used to make and reinforce specific points. An example might be: Nzinga not only fought against the forces of slavery in Angola for more than 50 years but had she not, there would have been a greater drain of people from Afrika to the new world, and the Afrikan population of the Americas would be much larger now. It is interesting to speculate whether, with greater numbers, Afrikan culture in the Americas would have been more intact than it is now.

Biography is, however, an excellent tool in ROPP. It should be made clear that biography is only a part of history. In Biography, the trainee can see himself/herself and realize the possibility of greatness. Biography can illustrate that many (if not most) of the problems faced by youth today are timeless, as are many (if not most) of the solutions. Biographies are an extension of the concept of role modeling.

Another good example of the use of biography for discussion and speculation would be the example of Denmark Vesey. What would have happened if his revolt had not occurred? What would have happened if he had been successful? What forces can make a person love their enslaver/oppressor more than they love their own people? Do you know any Denmark Veseys? Do you know any traitors who would betray their own people? The discussion possibilities are tremendous but should be contextual rather than episodic.

Experiential

From the discussion of Great Afrikans from the past, connect lines to show that you know who did what. These individuals should have been touched on in the didactic part.

1. Brave Ashanti Queen, mother who fought the British	Granville Woods
2. Father of Black Nationalism	Martin Delany
3. Female journalist who campaigned against lynching	Mary McLeod Bethune
4. Did the first open-heart surgery	Yaa Asantewa
5. The first Pharaoh	Garret Morgan
6. The first woman to do public speaking in America	Daniel Hale Williams
7. Civil Rights pioneer who started Association of Negro Women	Harriet Tubman
8. Charleston, SC slave revolt planner	Maria Stewart
9. Organized a college out of a garbage dump	Imhotep
10. First known physician and multi genius	Hatshepsut
11. Afrikan female king	Narmer
12. "Black Moses" of the Underground Railroad	Denmark Vesey
13. Invented the stoplight	Ida B. Wells Barnett

14. Invented railway telegraphy   Dorothy Height

Media

Sankofa

The video Sankofa deals with a woman who has tried to forget the past history of her people. Through a trick of fate, she has to face and relive that past. The video is both real and symbolic. Question what does Sankofa mean? How could so few keep so many in slavery? What does it mean when people say the snake will eat what's in the belly of the frog? Is the old man Sankofa really crazy? Why does the woman come out of the old slave castle naked? What are all the people looking at, at the end of the movie? Was she really reborn? What does it mean to be reborn?

Out of Darkness

Field Trip

Any Afrikan-oriented museum or exhibit or business that can speak or show African artifacts or artifacts from the past.

References and Suggested Reading for Unit Two

Adams, Russell (see References from Unit One)

Akbar, Na'im. *Chains and Images of Psychological Slavery,* Jersey City: New Mind Productions, 1984

Browder, Anthony T. *Exploding the Myths, Volume 1: Nile Valley Contributions to Civilizations,* Washington: The Institute of Karmic Guidance, 1992

Browder, Anthony T. *Egypt on the Potomac: A Guide to Decoding Egyptian Architecture and Symbols in Washington, D.C.* Washington: The Institute of Karmic Guidance, 2004

Clarke, John Henrik: *African People in World History,* Baltimore: Black Classic Press, , MD

Clarke, John Henrik. *Notes for an African World Revolution: Africans at the Crossroads,* Trenton:Africa World Press, 1991

Diop, Cheikh Anta. *African Origins of Civilization: Myth or Reality,* Westport: Lawrence Hill and Company, 1974

Haber, Louis. *Black Pioneers of Science and Invention,* NY: Harcourt Brace Jovanovich Publishers, 1970

Houston, Druscilla Dungee. *Those Wonderful Ethiopians of the Kushite Empire.* Baltimore: Black Classic Press, 1985

Jackson, John G. *Introduction to African Civilizations,* Secaucus: The Citadel Press, 1970

Rogers, J.A. *Africa's Gift to America,* St. Petersburg, FL: Helga M. Rogers, 1961

Stuckey, Sterling. *Slave Culture: Nationalist Theory and the Foundations of Black America,* NY: Oxford University Press, 1987

Van Sertima, Ivan has edited the *Journal of African Civilizations* for several years. Several issues of that publication, which is published by Transaction Books in New Brunswick, NJ, are particularly appropriate here:
African Presence in Early Europe

Egypt Revisited
Black Women in Antiquity
Blacks in Science: Ancient and Modern
African Presence in Early Asia
African Presence in Early America
Great Black Leaders: Ancient and Modern
Egypt: Child of Africa (includes Nile Valley Civilizations)
Great African Thinkers
Golden Age of the Moor

Watkins, Valethia

Williams, Chancellor. *The Destruction of Black Civilization: Great Issues of a Race from 4500 B.C. to 2000 A.D.* Chicago: Third World Press, 1976

Unit Three

"We'll Learn Ya,' Durn Ya"

Afrikan Education: Values

"The role and purpose of education is to allow each generation in society to rationally guide and systematically guarantee that it reproduces and refines the best of itself and by so doing, pass on to the next generation its accumulated wisdom, and the knowledge and skills necessary to develop, maintain and participate in the society of the future."

-Wade W. Nobles, Ph.D.

One of the main benefits of Afrikan Centered Rites of Passage Programs is that they provide a value system that is "tried and true" over thousands of years. Too often today, people try to solve perceived problems with variations of the same old tired remedies that have always failed. Our Ancestors tell us that there are several approaches to the question of values and that they can all be useful in the lives of all people.

The following values are Afrikan systems that have been created by ancient and contemporary Afrikan people. They are not being suggested to the exclusion of anything else, but in an Afrikan Centered system, Afrikan systems must be used.

Our ancient Afrikan Ancestors, the Kamieu, of the area now known as Egypt, believed in one Great God. This God was so great that It was unknowable. They contented themselves to learn all the positive principles of God. Maat was the female wisdom principle of God. It was the oldest principle, one that ensured the Godly order of reality. The

Principles of Maat were the guiding force by which all things were governed and the glue that kept divine order in man. The ancients believed that adherence to these principles guaranteed them a place in Paradise after death. To attempt to achieve as much perfection as possible was of utmost importance. Education prepared the student to live a good, just, righteous and productive life in the eyes of God and man. This type of education revolved around a group of Cardinal Virtues that each student (Initiate) had to master in order to proceed to the next level. This was a lifetime process, and the basics could take as long as thirty years to master.

Material gain was NOT considered important enough to be included in the goals of education. The teaching of character was inherent in this system of education. In this Afrikan system, level of education, morals and ethics, and material gain were related; however, in the Western system of education, there is no relationship between level of education and morals and ethics. The socialization associated with the western system of education continues to have material gain as an inherent value and goal.

Instead of each generation improving upon the accumulated wisdom and knowledge of the previous generation, as stated by Dr. Nobles in the quote leading off the chapter, the net results are a degeneration of morals and ethics with each succeeding generation. This results in each generation acknowledging that the education received by their children is inferior to the education that they received.

The Declarations of Innocence (called by some "The Negative Confessions") are believed to be more than 5000 years old. They were used by our Kemetic Ancestors at Judgment Day. They believed that when one died, at Judgment, in front of God, the Netchers (angels, Pillars, Orishas or aspects of God), and one's Ancestors, one had to be able to recite these Affirmations of a rightly lived life. When one could truthfully recite these Affirmations, the heart became as light as the feather of Maat. Then the Son of God would lead the deceased to the Father (God), who, in turn, would allow the deceased to pass into Paradise.

Finally, the Nguzo Saba are principles created by an Afrikan American intellectual, Dr. Maulana Karenga of Los Angeles, California. One of the key elements of a rites of passage program is to introduce Afrikan value systems. The Principles of Maat, the Virtues, and the Nguzo Saba should be committed to memory. However, it is through daily practice that these values become part of a personality. Maat occurs whether a person practices them or not. Maat is natural law and is uncontrollable by humans. For example, no matter how hard we try, the human mind cannot indefinitely remember a lie. The very nature of all in nature strives to fulfill Maat. How we learn to fulfill Maat is by mastering the Virtues and Nguzo Saba. At our final judgment, the book of life measures us by the standards of the Declarations of Innocence. An individual becomes a blessing to his family and community if the practices of Maat, the Virtues, and Nguzo Saba are followed.

When studying this area, it is good to allow time for general discussion. We recommend gearing these discussions around the various maxims in the book, *The Teachings of Ptahhotep: The Oldest Book in the World*, translated by Asa Hilliard, Larry Obadele Williams, and Nia Damali. Even though this book is thousands of years old, it relates perfectly to the lives and experiences of today's Afrikan youth. We cannot overemphasize just how important we feel this book to be in Afrikan Centered Rites of Passage.

The Principles of Maat

TRUTH

The truth is the opposite of a lie. The human mind was created in such a way that it cannot keep or remember a lie. Truth crushed to earth will always rise. We must always strive to seek, know, and speak truth at all times. If our goal is to achieve a world where all people strive for truth in all things, we can surpass the spiritual achievement of our Ancestors.

When our youth become known as respecters of the truth, they will experience respect from both their peers and elders. The untruthful fear the truth. Our youth must also learn that there is no one and nothing important enough to compromise themselves by telling untruths.

JUSTICE

Justice is doing what is right and treating people fairly. If you do right, people will do right by you. If one does wrong, divine justice (called "karma" by many people) occurs, and one has to suffer the consequences of their actions. Even if justice does not appear to occur, Divine justice is always exacted.

Many of our young people already have a well-developed sense of fairness. Unfortunately, too often, it is not positively reinforced at school, at home or even at church or mosque. The value of justice must be reinforced so that they will not be reluctant to be just. They must realize that justice is its own reward and is part of the Divine Order of reality.

Our youth must learn to do the right thing because it is the right thing to do and not because of fear or an expected reward. This can be easily learned when there is a love of self and others.

RIGHTEOUSNESS

Being and doing right is always best. Sometimes doing right may appear to be costly because wrongdoing sometimes appears to be profitable. To see others who have done wrong and have temporarily profited from that wrong will, at times, make us question doing right. However, the righteous or right doing people understand that deeds that need to be hidden should not be done; words that cannot be shared with others should not be spoken.

The righteous cooperate with that which is good for themselves, their families, and their communities. They oppose that which is destructive. The righteous love peace and acting peacefully. They love people. The actions of the righteous draw others to them and to Maat.

HARMONY

A choir is made up of many voices. If they work together, the resulting sound becomes as one but greater than each single voice. The same principle applies to life. We can accomplish much if we work together. No goal is out of reach for those who are united in harmony. We must help our young people to understand how much better the world will be if Afrikan people can achieve harmony sufficient to introduce Afrikan values and ethics in one voice.

BALANCE

Each person must be balanced mentally, physically, and spiritually. To be unbalanced mentally is to be crazy. To be unbalanced physically is to be weak. To be unbalanced spiritually is to be foolish. There should always be balance between the seen (material things) and the unseen (the spiritual and the metaphysical), between work and play and between service and reward.

Today's reality is profoundly out of balance in favor of the superficial and the material. Our youth are bombarded with messages that subvert balance. We must teach them not only to consider balance, but to seek it.

ORDER

This is always a right sequence in doing things. Two should always follow one, and three always come after two. A person should always work before he plays and rest after each.

There is a Divine Order inherent in all things. Our Ancestors strenuously sought to recognize and live within this Divine Order. Our youth have the potential to advance the understanding of the Divine Order of things even beyond where our Ancestors left it.

PROPRIETY

There is a proper way to carry yourself, address others and, indeed, to do all things. We must always strive to be appropriate in all that we do. Propriety is the respect of the proper way.

There are different ways of dressing and communicating that are all useful and helpful depending on the circumstances. The ability to choose that which is appropriate must be ingrained into our youth. Then, hip-hop dress, Ebonics and slang will not be used at a job interview.

RECIPROCITY

"Do unto others as you would have them do unto you." "What goes around comes around (Karma)." Reciprocity is the Golden Rule of all religions and philosophies of life. If our youth display the consideration needed in adhering to this principle, they will be leaders and role models.

There were also other principles that were very important in ancient, pre-Arabic and pre-European Afrika. These were:

EXCELLENCE

It was believed that everyone should do their best in everything they attempt. No matter what the circumstances, only your best will do. If you failed in anything, no one can blame you for failure if you did your best. "Anything worth doing at all is worth doing well" (Afrikan proverb). The Afrikan youth of today rarely live up to their true potential.

A major goal of Rites of Passage is to condition our youth to always do their best, even without thinking about it. "*Strive for Excellence in all you do so that no fault can be found in your character*" (Ptahhotep in *The Book of Coming Forth by Day: The Ethics of the Declarations of Innocence,* University of Sankore Press, Los Angeles, 1990, p.28).

HONOR

It was believed that one's actions reflected not only on the individual but also on the family, community, and nation. Therefore, one was asked to act only in a manner of respect and dignity that would make the community proud.

LOYALTY

Everyone has to be loyal to someone and something. The chain of loyalty was to family, community, and race. When this chain was finally broken, the Maafa began. Our youth must realize that there are relative loyalties and ultimate loyalties. The loyalty to our community and race is not to be compromised. *"A white dog does not bite another white dog"* (Afrikan proverb).

SERVICE

No matter what type of work is done by a person, that person should do good for others. The importance of providing service to one's community and race was still realized long after our Ancestors were kidnapped, enslaved and brought to America. In fact, until only several years ago, it was taught that to help someone was one of the most important things that a person could do.

COURAGE

Knowing the right thing to do is not enough. It is frequently harder to do the right thing than it is to do the wrong thing. A person should have the courage to do the right thing even if his/her friends are doing wrong and urging him/her to do wrong.

RESPECT

Respect is the bedrock of a stable society. Respect always begins with respect for self. When one has respect for oneself, respecting others naturally follows.

RESPONSIBILITY

We all have several layers of duties and responsibilities: to self, to family, to community, to the nation and to race. Frequently, they are interrelated. All things function effectively if all people are responsible.

Cardinal Virtues Sought by Students in Ancient Afrika

Control of Thought

Today's world is full of distractions. Our youth are immersed in many temptations. Practicing the concept of control of thought will provide our youth with the tools to overcome the distractions and temptations with which they are faced.

Control of Action

Once one is able to control his or her thoughts, it is only natural that actions are controlled. The aim of the Cardinal Virtues is to assure that those actions are positive or appropriate.

Devotion of Purpose

It is very easy to give up. Indeed, many of our young people display their giving up in many ways, from violence against those who look like them to failing in school and in life. Rites of Passage training teaches them that they should be true to any task that they attempt, especially those that better themselves, their families and their communities. Our youth must learn that the completion of a task is as important as the attempt.

Faith in the teacher's ability to teach the truth

Those who have fallen victim to the evils of today's world tend to victimize vulnerable people. Our youth are well aware of this and frequently have more than the usual suspicion of those in older generations. Our Ancestors' system was based on inherent faith in adults, both educationally and morally. By example, the trainer has to prove his/her trustworthiness to the trainee and the student will be able to envision what faith in an elder/teacher is about.

Faith in one's ability to know the truth

The damage done to our youth includes self-doubt in their ability to learn. They are made to believe that they cannot learn as well as others. Consequently, they frequently don't even try or readily accept grades and evaluations that do not represent their ability. Rites of Passage training in value systems is geared to remove this self-doubt.

Faith in one's ability to use the truth

Too often, the confidence of our young people has been taken. This occurs in many ways. What internalizing the value system of our Ancestors does it build confidence in oneself and one's ability to perform those tasks that are needed.

Freedom from resentment under persecution

Given the history of the recent Afrikan presence in America, it is difficult to avoid bitterness. Our Ancestors were not only enslaved but persecuted and subjected to the most brutal system of suppression and oppression (the Maafa) in the annals of world history. It is important that our youth be told repeatedly that resentment stunts growth. One cannot function effectively and efficiently with any type of resentment. When one is free from resentment under persecution, the Maatian Law of Reciprocity enables positivity to dominate any situation.

Freedom from resentment when wronged

This relates to the previous Virtue. Afrikan people have been wronged systematically over the last several hundred years. Maatian ethics teaches us that we should not attempt to artificially exact retribution. The Maatian principles of Balance, Order and Reciprocity will prevail. What we do need to do is continue to follow the principles/values left for us by our Ancestors. One cannot move forward while trying to hold someone back or while trying to exact revenge.

Ability to distinguish right from wrong

The relativity of Western values has made this a major problem. In ancient Afrika, politicians might get the death penalty just because politicians have to compromise truth. Our task now is to teach our youth to recognize truth. We must recognize how difficult this is.

Ability to distinguish the real from the unreal

With the expertise of those in advertising, almost anything can be sold. The power of illusion transcends understanding. Our youth and our adults are susceptible to the most powerful method of brainwashing and manipulation known to man. They must be given defense against this destructive power.

The Declaration of Innocence (Negative Confessions)

The Declarations of Innocence are just as old as the Principles of Maat and the Cardinal Virtues. If a person lived by Maat and the Virtues, it was assumed that at the final judgment, he or she could truthfully stand and recite their innocence of evil and evil behavior. Please note the resemblance between the Declarations of Innocence and the Ten Commandments. Remember that the Declarations are much older than the Ten Commandments and were part of the required curriculum learned by Moses in Kemet (Ancient Egypt).

1. I have not done iniquity (evil).
2. I have not robbed with violence.
3. I have not stolen.
4. I have done no murder; I have done no harm.
5. I have not defrauded offerings (destroyed food supplies).
6. I have not minished oblations (done fraudulent things).
7. I have not plundered the god (stolen sacred property).
8. I have spoken no lies.
9. I have not snatched away food.
10. I have not caused pain.
11. I have not committed fornication.
12. I have not caused shedding of tears.
13. I have not dealt deceitfully.
14. I have not transgressed (violated the law).
15. I have not acted guilefully (been a schemer).
16. I have not laid waste the ploughed land (stolen cultivated land).
17. I have not been an eavesdropper.
18. I have not set my lips in motion (against my man).
19. I have not been angry and wrathful except for a just cause.
20. I have not defiled the wife of any man (committed adultery).
21. I have not defiled the wife of any man (committed adultery).
22. I have not polluted myself.
23. I have not caused terror.
24. I have not transgressed.

25. I have not burned with rage (Been hot-tempered).
26. I have not stopped my ears against the words of Right and Truth.
27. I have not worked grief. (Taken advantage of vulnerable people.)
28. I have not acted with insolence.
29. I have not stirred up strife.
30. I have not judged hastily (been impatient).
31. I have not been an eavesdropper.
32. I have not multiplied words exceedingly (been too talkative).
33. I have done neither harm nor ill.
34. I have never cursed the king.
35. I have never fouled the water.
36. I have not spoken scornfully (raised my voice).
37. I have never cursed God.
38. I have not stolen.
39. I have not defrauded the offerings of the gods.
40. I have not plundered the offerings to the blessed dead.
41. I have not filched the food of the infant, neither have I sinned against the god of my native town.
42. I have not slaughtered with evil intent the cattle of the gods.

Nguzo Saba
(The Seven Principles)

The most recent addition to the philosophy and value system of Afrikans is the Nguzo Saba. Dr. Maulana Karenga, through studies of ancient Afrikan culture, rituals, and celebrations has developed what is popularly called Kwanzaa. Kwanzaa has gained widespread acceptance, and in 1997, the U.S. Postal Service commissioned a Kwanzaa stamp.

The basic principles of Kwanzaa are the Nguzo Saba, or Seven Principles. During Kwanzaa week, a candle is lit daily to represent one of the Principles. These principles are as follows:

UMOJA (Unity)
To strive for and maintain unity in the family, community, nation, and race.

KUJICHAGULIA (Self-determination)
To define ourselves, name ourselves, create for ourselves and speak for ourselves instead of being defined, named, created for, and spoken for by others.

UJIMA (Collective Work and Responsibility)
To build and maintain our community together and make our sisters' and brothers' problems our problems and to solve them together.

UJAMAA (Cooperative Economics)
To build and maintain our own stores, shops, and other businesses and to profit from them together.

NIA (Purpose)
To make our collective vocation the building and developing of our community in order to restore our people to their traditional greatness.

KUUMBA (Creativity)
To do always as much as we can, in the way we can, in order to leave our community more beautiful and beneficial than we inherited it.

IMANI (Faith)
To believe with all our heart in our people, our parents, our teachers, our leaders and the righteousness and victory of our struggle.

Materials Needed:	Same as previous Units
Didactic:	Brief discussions: The Principles of Maat Other African Values The Cardinal Virtues The Declarations of Innocence
Experiential:	Application of Maat Alligator River
Media:	Just Another Girl on the IRT South Central Heavy is the Crown, Vol. 1
Biography:	Carter G. Woodson Mary McLeod Bethune

Field trip: A trip to historically Black schools and colleges in the area, giving history of those institutions. It would be ideal to have older people participate in the tour and give their own experiences, memories and observations of those institutions. A trip to Tuskegee is optimal because of the Carver museum, the cemetery and all the history around the campus.

Literature: *"When you control a man's thinking, you do not have to worry about his actions. You do not have to tell him not to stand here or go yonder. He will find his 'proper place' and will stay in it. You do not need to send him to the back door. He will go without being told. In fact, if there is no back door, he will cut one for his special benefit. His education makes it necessary."*

Carter G. Woodson
Miseducation of the Negro

Expected Outcome: Upon completion of this Unit, the trainees will become more introspective. They will, hopefully, relate their lives and experiences and those of their friends/peers to the things that they have been exposed to and reevaluate the values they have had and been exposed to previously. The idea of hypocrisy will become more pronounced in their minds. They will become critical of some double standards that they have been exposed to and will encounter.

Didactic

One of the key elements of the ROPP is to introduce Afrikan value systems. The Principles of Maat, the Virtues, and the Nguzo Saba should be committed to memory. However, it is through daily practice that these values become part of a personality. Maat occurs whether a person practices them or not. Maat is natural law and is uncontrollable by humans. For example, no matter how hard we try, the human mind cannot remember a lie. The very nature of all in nature strives to fulfill Maat. How we learn to fulfill Maat is by mastering the Virtues and Nguzo Saba. At our final judgment, the book of life measures us by the standards of the Declarations of Innocence. An individual becomes a blessing to his family and community if the practices of Maat, the Virtues and Nguzo Saba are followed.

Experiential

Alligator River: Lost Love

There once was a girl named Shanikwa who loved a boy named Jamaal. Shanikwa lived on one side of a river infested with alligators, and water moccasins and Jamaal lived on the other side. One day a great storm came along and destroyed the only bridge which crossed the river. Shanikwa wanted to see Jamaal because she loved him so much but had no way of getting across the river. Shanikwa, in her desperation, went to see Dante, the only person who had a boat on her side of the river. Dante agreed to take Shanikwa across the river in his boat if she would go to bed with him. (For younger adolescents or children, use "Dante asked Shanikwa to steal a CD player from Wal-Mart or Best Buy). Shanikwa refused and went to see her best friend named Wes. Shanika told Wes how much she loved Jamaal and told Wes what Dante had asked her to do. Before Shanikwa could say another word, Wes told her that he did not want to be involved and walked away.

Shanikwa then decided to do what Dante asked. After she fulfilled her part of the deal, Dante rode Shanikwa on his boat across the river to see Jamaal. Dante further agreed to wait for Shanikwa for the return trip at no additional cost. Shanikwa went to see Jamaal at his home. When Jamaal opened the door, Shanikwa told him the whole story that has been told to you. Jamaal became angry and told Shanikwa that he never wanted to see her again. Shanikwa returned to the boat, and Dante sailed her back to their side of the river.

When Shanikwa left the dock, she was crying, and a big muscle-bound lug named Butch passed by. Butch asked her why she was crying, and she explained the whole story to him. Butch became mad and went to see Dante. Butch demanded that Dante take him across the river, and Dante agreed. Upon arriving on Jamaal's side of the river, Butch went to Jamaal's house. When Jamaal opened the door, Butch grabbed him and threw him off the porch. Butch then punched and kicked Jamaal, giving him a black eye and a broken arm in the process. Butch then returned with Dante across the river. Upon seeing Shanikwa, Butch told her what he had done. As this story ends, you can see Shanikwa walking off into the sunset, saying HA! HA!

Steps to complete the exercise

1. Number your paper from 1 through 5 (optimally, this should be done on a chalkboard or flipchart)
2. With 1 being your favorite character and 5 being what you consider the worse.
3. Divide trainees into two or three groups.
4. These groups are to come up with one list of rank-ordered characters. Group members are encouraged to talk with one another and to select a spokesperson for the group.
5. Once this task is completed, compare each group's final lists and write them side-by-side on a flip chart.
6. It will be interesting to hear the opinions of the groups and explore their reasons for choosing as they did. This is a tremendous teaching moment.

Brief Lecture

Each person in the story represents characteristics and values.

- Shanikwa represents unrequited and unconditional love, instigation, impulsiveness, naiveté and revenge.
- Dante represents the type of person who will do for you if you do for him first, keeps his word, adapts to situations and takes advantage.
- Wes represents friends who are not really friends and those who choose not to get involved.
- Butch is the unsolicited protector, the illogical brute, the impulsive avenger of something he had no part or involvement, a troublemaker.

We meet these kinds of people every day. The goal of the Rites of Passage Program is to teach how to avoid being one of these characters. The trainees' understanding of Maat and the other sets of Afrikan value systems should teach them how each one of the characters in the story should have behaved.

Media

Several videos selected for this unit illustrate Maat and the Virtues in day-to-day modern life. At this point, dependent upon your group's composition, you may want to split the boys from the girls. *South Central* is designed to give boys an understanding of character, and *Just Another Girl of the IRT* is designed for girls. Both videos are quite graphic, and the language is the language of the streets, which our children hear daily.

The point of the videos hits home hard to older adolescents. If your group is very young, you may want to use Lion King as a substitution. Do not get hung up on the content of the videos. Preview them so that you can understand the intent. Compare the intent with Maat, the Virtues and the other characteristics you are trying to teach. Other videos that are helpful to this unit are *Avatar, The Egg of Life, Akeelah and the Bee, Glory Road, Their Eyes Were Watching God, Drum Line* and *Hotel Rwanda.*

Field Trips

Field trips to colleges, community colleges, or universities that are either Historically Black or cater to large numbers of Black students are suggested. Getting trainees interested in going to further education is important and exposing them to collegiate environments is a step toward building the expectation to attend. Arrange for them to talk with students, interested faculty or staff at the college.

References and Suggested Reading for Unit Three

Akoto, Kwame Agyei. *Nationbuilding: Theory and Practice in Afrikan Centered Education,* Washington: Pan Afrikan World Institute, 1992

Budge, E.A. Wallis. *The Egyptian Book of the Dead,* NY: Dover Publications, Inc.,1967 (pp. 347-349)

Carruthers, Jacob H. *Essays in Ancient Egyptian Studies,* Los Angeles: University of Sankore Press, 1984

Hilliard, Asa G. III, Larry Williams, Nia Damali (Editors) *The Teachings of Ptahhotep: The Oldest Book in the World,* Atlanta: Blackwood Press and Co., Inc., 1987

James, George G.M. *Stolen Legacy,* San Francisco: Julian Richardson Associates, 1954

Karenga, Maulana. *Selections from the Husia: Sacred Wisdom of Ancient Egypt.* Los Angeles: University of Sankore Press, 1984

Karenga, Maulana. *The African American Holiday of Kwanzaa: A Celebration of Family, Community, and Culture,* Los Angeles: University of Sankore Press, 1989

Karenga, Maulana. *The Book of Coming Forth by Day.* Los Angeles: University of Sankore Press, 1990

Opoku, Kofi Asare. *West African Traditional Religion,* Accra: Fep International Private, Limited, 1978

Richards, Dona Marimba. *Let the Circle Be Unbroken: The Implications of African Spirituality in the Diaspora,* Trenton: The Red Sea Press, 1990

Woodson, Carter G. *The Mis-Education of the Negro,* Washington: The Associated Publishers, 1933

Unit Four

"Making the Right Choices"

Problem Solving and Decision Making

Afrikan Leadership Development

"Free your mind, and your (butt) will follow."

- George Clinton

A major part of Rites of Passage is the development of future leaders. The Cardinal Virtues mentioned previously were designed to produce servant leaders. They were taught to make the right decision at the right time. Leadership, therefore, is a combination of Right Thinking, Right Planning and Right Doing.

Everything that we currently have and will ever have is a result of how we use our minds. You are what you think about all the time. It is with the use of our minds that we develop a purpose for living. Thinking and following up on those things we think about prepares us for today and the future.

Most people use only a fraction of their thinking power. Yet, how well you think will far outweigh your ability to use your physical abilities in the future. Most people spend a great deal of time worrying rather than thinking and others avoid thinking and just act upon their emotions. Most people have never learned how to think.

Developing the ability to think and set goals is very important to the solution of problems.

Thinking takes discipline, and discipline simply means "doing within while you are doing without." When a person is properly prepared, then those things that she or he wants will come. The beginning of all pain in human life is wanting and having things. However, if the time is right and a person is prepared, things wanted can be obtained with a minimum of suffering.

In addition to the ability to think, it is necessary to have a plan based upon a purpose. Too often, Afrikan people have relied upon fate or circumstance to dictate action. Yet, planning should be involved in all that we do. As children, we have all been asked what our future goals will be ("What do you want to be when you grow up?"). We would struggle and then say something to please the adult who asked the question. Not knowing was an honest answer. It seems strange to come in contact with adults who have no idea of what they are becoming. Considering these adults, it is no wonder that many Afrikan teenagers struggle with the question when asked.

This lack of knowledge and, more specifically, lack of planning leads to many of the failures in the Afrikan community in America. Thirty years after the riots in Newark, New Jersey, the city still looked almost the same as the day after the riots, as did New Orleans five years after Hurricane Katrina. Newark seemed to be a city with a majority Afrikan population, a series of Afrikan mayors, and no plan for the future. Newark is a constant visual example of what the lack of planning can produce, but what planning can achieve.

On a personal level, the lack of planning and setting goals is even more crucial. The average American of Afrikan descent will attend several large weddings in a lifetime and hear about numerous divorces. Divorce or abandonment have become a way of life in our community. This was not the Afrikan way and did not become our way until we traded in our Afrikan systems for the systems of others. Let us look at the process, and we can readily observe the mistake.

The wedding is usually a beautiful ceremony. Much planning goes into successful weddings. Decisions such as which foot from which to lead, the size of the cake, the band for the reception, the rewriting of vows, which songs to include and who will sing them, the colors and other items too numerous to mention are painstakingly detailed and planned. On the day of the wedding, there are usually a few "hitches," but for the most part, the wedding comes off as planned.

On the other hand, too frequently, little or no thought has occurred regarding the marriage. Major decisions, such as when or if to have children, who handle the household money, who takes off when the children are sick, and other things too numerous to mention are rarely, if ever, discussed in any meaningful depth. The question is, what is more important, the wedding, which lasts about an hour, or the marriage, which should last a lifetime? The answer is obvious, but actions taken by many Afrikan people demonstrate that this question is not considered. The results have been disastrous. Nearly seventy percent of all Afrikan children will grow up in a household with one parent, usually without a father.

As a result of racism, oppression, and poor economics are cited as the cause for the breakup of Afrikan families, the lack of clear goals and planning may be a more important and underlying factor. If a wedding can come off smoothly, so can a marriage. If planning and setting goals made the wedding work, then planning and goal setting can make a marriage work.

In the process of thinking, discipline is necessary in planning and putting the plan in action. All of us need thinking time. The Afrikan way is to share thoughts and formulate plans from as much positive input as possible.

Project: Sankofa suggests that true happiness, success, and wealth require a collective effort and anything that requires effort requires the involvement of others. These are merely suggestions and may not pertain to your personal life, but thinking and planning are essential to gaining happiness, success, and wealth.

Planning calls for thinking about the future. What are your personal, professional, and academic goals? These goals should be written and reviewed periodically to measure how far you have come and how much further you have toward achieving what you want. Steps to achieve the goals should be clear, and, if truly thought out, dates for reaching the goals should be set.

There is nothing more important than a person's life. Where that life is headed is of equal importance. If a life is so important, it needs to be put at the head of all planning and goal setting. It should be planned as carefully as your wedding or your next vacation.

When confronted with a problem, most people usually approach it in either of three ways: they make excuses, run from them, or solve them. At issue in the Afrikan community is that two of the three methods are not acceptable. For too many years, we have made excuses for the problems found in our community. For example, bad or misguided behavior is attributed to racism. Of course, racism is one of the obstacles that presents itself in the American environment. However, there are too many within the Afrikan community who have thrived despite racism for it to be the cause of so many problems. An ill-prepared worker cannot blame racism for poor performance on a job. A student who does not study or do homework cannot blame racism for bad grades. A poor attitude will get poor results regardless of the amount of racism encountered.

There was a time in America for Afrikans when running from a problem was not a bad move. That time was during slavery. In many life-threatening situations, running is the only alternative. Fortunately, most problems are not life-threatening and should be dealt with in a manner that yields the best results. Most problems do not call for snap judgments. However, using the African value systems (e.g., Maat and the Virtues) leads to amazingly positive outcomes.

If used in "order", the Virtues (a Principle of Maat) has a calming effect. Thought, action, and purpose are the proper order for dealing with problems. Generally, what worsens problems is action taken before thought is given. This is usually followed by an apology.

To modernize the Virtues for use in today's world, the SARA approach to solving problems is used in Project Sankofa's Rites of Passage Program. SARA is an acronym for scanning, analysis, reaction, and assessment.

Scanning means looking for a specific question or problem.

Analysis is a fancy word that includes the five "Ws" (who, what, when, where, and why) plus how. Once we think about a problem, it is easier to confront the issues involved. How we deal with the problem and come to the right decision to solve the problem leads to a reference point to begin our action.

Normally when we are dealing with a problem, it is reaction rather than true action. The Rites of Passage Program is a reaction to the continued cries about the plight of Afrikan children. It also reacts to the helplessness, which is expressed verbally and behaviorally by adults seeking solutions to this continuous problem. Rites of Passage programs are also proactive in that they provide methods of seeking to create the best people possible.

Finally, when the reaction is completed, an assessment should occur to see if the desired results occurred. Again, using the Rites of Passage Program, an assessment occurs following each step in the process and after its completion.

The Program has evolved after each training due to the trainers gaining more insight into the problems of youth and adults today.

This final part of the problem-solving process is essential. No program is a solution unto itself. A living and evolving approach leads to better results. Methods that can be used in both the personal and programmatic world have a tendency to be integrated into the personality of the user and those being trained. This is important because the program becomes more effective if the trainers truly believe in it. The methods used in a Rites of Passage Program should be a way of life for all involved.

Materials needed: Same as previous Units

Didactic Instruction: Brief discussion on problem-solving and decision making.

Experiential: Components of successful decision-making:

a. Observation is using the five senses and intuition to correctly recognize what is happening.
b. Description is making sure that the observation is correctly perceived and can be verbalized or written.
c. Formulation is the analysis of the observation and description combined with a plan of action. Part of this step is deciding on a plan of action or whether any action is necessary.
d. Implementation is performing the plan of action.
e. Evaluation is seeing the results of your actions, i.e., whether the problem was resolved. Occasionally, one may need to go through all five components again (Stop, Think, Act, Review).

Media: Vernon Johns
The Drop Squad

Biography: Malcolm X
Ida B. Wells Barnett
Paul Robeson
Muhammad Ali
Nzinga
Curt Flood

Field Trip: Visit Black businesses, attorneys and social workers and discuss the decisions and problems that they face daily.

Literature: *We Wear the Mask* by Paul Lawrence Dunbar. What does this poem mean in terms of deception? In this case, did deception relate to survival? Is the basic idea of the poem outdated in today's world? What is being "fake"? What are "shape shifters"?

Expected Outcome: Trainees will develop the ability to properly assess problems and then make decisions based on that assessment, thus reducing impulsive behavior.

Didactic

All people have what we call problems. Unfortunately, problems are usually not always solved. If we think of problems as questions, then all a person has to do is answer the question. Another way of thinking about this is to think of what we call world problems such as hunger or war. There have always been hunger and war, and the best minds of all generations have worked on the problems of hunger and war.

Yet, with all of their thinking power, no solution has been developed. However, what happens if you formulate these problems into questions? Why does hunger exist? In reality, there is more food in the world than there are people to eat it. How can we get the food to people who are hungry? Is food a privilege or a right for all people? As you can see, questions will generate the proper dialog towards solutions. Problems, on the other hand, suggest permanency and normalcy rather than suggesting solutions.

Frequently, in approaching problems, the wrong questions are asked. If one asks the wrong question, it is fairly certain that he/she will get the wrong answer. It is important to always double check to see if you are asking correct and pertinent questions.

When confronted with a problem, people usually feel that they have three choices in how to deal with them. People make excuses, run from them, or solve them. ROPP teaches the approach to solving problems.

The trainers should present situations for the students to evaluate and discuss their thoughts.

Experiential

SARA Model

After hearing a brief lecture on Observation, Description, Formulation, Implementation, and Evaluation, each trainee should be directed to write in large letters:

S A R A

The "S" stands for scanning. Scanning means looking for a specific question or problem. Often, if we scale down and define our question correctly, we can solve the problem and answer the question. Never try to solve many problems or answer many questions at one time. Scanning allows us to pick the first question that needs to be answered.

The "A" stands for analysis. Analysis is a fancy word that includes the five "Ws" (who, what, when, where, why) plus "how" and "how often." The "A" allows you to formulate an answer to the question or problem.

The "R" stands for how you react to the problem or question. Reacting without scanning or analysis leads to trouble. Thus, order, which is one of the Principles of Maat, comes into play. Reacting to a problem should always follow scanning and analysis.

The final "A" stands for assessment. Assessment is looking back to see if how you reacted was appropriate and if it got the results that you intended or wanted. Assessment is an excellent measure of how to learn. If your reaction to the problem was wrong, what did you learn? If things worked out well, what did you learn?

The "SARA" model is an easy method to use to think through problems.

Media

The videos for this unit demonstrate how in fiction (*Drop Squad*) and in true life (*Vernon Johns*), problems are solved through a rational process. Utilize the experiential materials and the didactic to formulate questions. You may want to compare the lessons learned in the two videos. Again, stopping the videos to discuss key points is important.

Field Trips

Field trips to local attorneys, black businesses, black newspapers, and other private resources to learn how they solve problems on a day-to-day basis. People who are confronted with daily obstacles provide personal testimony that problems can be overcome.

References and Suggested Reading for Unit Four

See previous reading lists

Unit Five

"I've Got a Plan"

Goal Setting and Thinking Skills
Luck is Being Prepared for Opportunity

This unit deals with developing the ability to think and set goals. Successful people think their way through to the solution of problems. They set goals and rigorously train their mind to achieve desired results. They constantly prepare themselves for the day or minute of opportunity. It is always better to be prepared for an opportunity and not have it than to have an opportunity and not be prepared. In fact, "luck" has been defined as being prepared for opportunity.

Thinking takes discipline. Discipline simply means doing from within while you are doing from without. When a person is properly prepared, then those things wanted will come. If the time is right and a person is prepared, then most things that they want (material and spiritual) can be obtained with a minimum of effort and suffering.

Materials needed:	Same as previous Units
Didactic:	Brief discussion on establishing goals: Why is goal-setting important? How do you set goals? Delayed gratification.
Media:	*Glory*
Biography:	John-Jacques Dessalines Hon. Marcus Mosiah Garvey Yaa Asantewa

Literature:	*If I Must Die* by Claude McKay What does this poem mean? Which of the values and virtues are covered in this poem? Evaluate each line of this poem. Analyze how it could be pertinent today.
Field Trip:	Civil War Site (In SC, Fort Moultrie in Charleston is an excellent place to visit after seeing the film *Glory*) Civil Rights Site (Civil Rights Museum in Memphis, the Martin Luther King site in Atlanta are only a few that can be chosen).
Expected Outcome:	To develop discipline and delayed gratification in the Trainees. They should be able to associate the relationship of sacrifice and patience to hard work and success.

Didactic

This unit deals with developing the ability to think and set goals. Successful people think their way through to the solution of problems. They set goals and rigorously train their mind to achieve desired results. They constantly prepare themselves for the day or minute of opportunity. It is always better to be prepared for an opportunity and not have it than to have an opportunity and not be prepared. In fact, "luck" has been defined as being prepared for opportunity."

Thinking takes discipline. Discipline simply means doing within while you are doing without. When a person is properly prepared, then those things wanted will come. The beginning of all pain in human life is wanting and having things. However, if the time is right and a person is prepared, then most things wanted (material and spiritual) can be obtained with a minimum of suffering.

Experiential

Exercise #1

Thinking Time - Each trainee is to pick a time of one hour when they will be free to think at home. At the top of a piece of paper, they are to label three columns: Happy, Successful, and Rich. Their assignment is to think of 5 ways under each heading that will make them more happy, successful or rich. This exercise is done to strengthen their mind using the value systems that will be discussed throughout the program.

HAPPY	SUCCESSFUL	RICH

Exercise #2

GOAL CHART

CATEGORY	ONE YEAR	TWO YEARS	THREE YEARS
Personal and Social Goals			
Academic Goals			
Employment Goals			

Signature of Trainee

Signature of Trainer

Date

References and Suggested Reading for Unit Five

Kuykendall, Crystal. *From Rage to Hope: Strategies for Reclaiming Black and Hispanic Students,* Bloomington: National Educational Service, 1992

Kunjufu, Jawanza. *Motivating and Preparing Black Youth to Work,* Chicago: African American Images, 1986

Majors, Richard and Janet Mancini Billson (previously cited after Introduction)

Nobles, Wade W., Lawford L., Goddard, William E. Cavil, III, and Pamela Y. George. *African-American Families: Issues, Insights and Directions,* Oakland: A Black Family Institute Publication, 1987

Unit Six

"Being Poor Ain't No Virtue"

Collective Economics

"They feed their children while ours starve."

-The authors

Economics is the study of human choices regarding the use of resources. Resources, in an economic sense, can be money, land, minerals, people, food, and other commodities that have value. The Afrikan community, whether on The Continent or in the United States, has a long history of having its resources pillaged and used for the accumulation of wealth of others. That so many Afrikans are economically disadvantaged in the United States is a visible example of the pillage because human beings are economic resources in an economic system.

Economics is also the study of the history of human relationships. How humans interact concerning resources is a major part of economics. In fact, if economics were taught from the human relations perspective, it would probably become the favorite topic in schools. However, the manner in which economics is taught leaves the student with little information to improve self or increase a personal knowledge base. The information is presented and provided to the student in such a manner that economics can be seen as being developed on another planet. Why teach this alien stuff, and what does economics have to do with Black people?

All knowledge should come from a social/cultural context and be usable in a personal context. Knowledge outside of this personal context is alienated knowledge. Thus, if the knowledge is alienated, it cannot be used by self.

This is important to know because it relates to economics as well as other fields related to economics. Is it not interesting that those who go to college, get degrees in business, business administration or even master's degrees in business seldom start or operate businesses? Alienated knowledge cannot be used to benefit oneself or one's people. For knowledge to be usable, it has to be connected to the structure and function of a people.

The structure and function of Afrikan people, for the last 300-500 years, has been to be pawns and resource commodities for other people. We have been a means for the enrichment of others in an economic system devised by others. In today's reality, our major economic function has been to be consumers. A group that only consumes, can only support others. Money is not a problem in the Afrikan community in the United States. The collective wealth (based upon earnings) makes AUSA the ninth or tenth richest nation on Earth. Yet, if you ask most people, the perception of Afrikans in the United States is one of poverty. So, our problem seems two-fold in the economic field.

First, we need to separate the real from the unreal (remember Afrikan values). AUSA are a people with money and no economic system. We were taught to use our money to enrich others by being consumers. More importantly, we enrich others so they can feed their children while our children starve. Our children starve for food, jobs, education, and good sense concerning economics.

The second economic truth is that relationships are built upon trust. However, a people who have been taught to mistrust each other cannot develop an economic system. AUSA put more trust in a people who have enslaved them, Jim Crowed them, disrespected them, oppressed them and abused them than in their own people. All newly arrived immigrants immediately pick up on this reality and begin building their wealth in Black communities. No one would put a business in an area where there is no money. Yet, even in the poorest sections of the Black community, you will find a fried chicken franchise and at least one Chinese restaurant. Our problem is not money, it is a matter of trust. If I do not trust you, then I will not spend money with you, cooperate with you, or help you financially.

We need an economic system as a people. We suffer, because we lack such a system. Systems existed before money was created. We have plenty of money and no way to hold on to it for the accumulation of wealth. A system is a way to use money to benefit self, family, and community. An economic system is a manner in which a people choose to relate to each other. If we choose to deal with each other in an atmosphere of mistrust, in a fragmented and disorganized manner, we will continue to get the same economic results. An economic system devised by AUSA differs from current capitalism due to the presence of trust. A truism in capitalism is "buyer beware".

If we pay close attention to those who seem to prosper in the United States, we notice that "correct English," MBAs from Harvard or Yale, and individual effort do not seem to be the prerequisites. Interestingly enough, many of the wealthiest people in America do not even have a college degree. In fact, those who prosper, especially in Black communities, speak the least English (newly arrived Chinese, Arabs, East Indians, Koreans, and Mexicans). They are high school or tech school graduates and seem to have excellent family support. Though many in the Black community are angered by the presence of these "foreigners" with businesses in the black community, it is fair to say that nearly 100% of their customers are from that same Black community. This type of anger is futile and nonproductive, and if we are angry, it should be at ourselves.

Anger is useless, however, unless it is directed toward a positive goal. The development of an African economic system is imperative. An Afrikan economic system has to be built upon trust. It would develop wealth and benefit from the redistribution of wealth systems of America. What is open to us, economically is the stock market and the means to understand how wealth is accumulated in America.

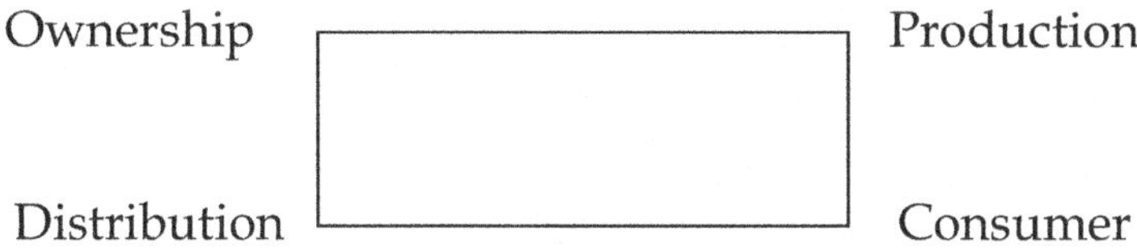

Wealth in the United States is directly related to business ownership, production, and distribution of goods and services. Consumption is the method of distributing money, which starts the process again. Ownership has the greatest risk associated with it; conversely, ownership also reaps the greatest reward. Production and distribution closely follow the risk and reward model of wealth. Consumers, basically, provide money and receive temporary services or goods. However, educated consumers can significantly and directly affect ownership, production, and distribution.

Ask yourself a question, "What if I had to be rich?" Would you not think differently about acquiring wealth? If you had to be rich, you would learn all there is to know about becoming wealthy. You would study not only the system but also those who prosper from the system. You would develop a personalized plan of action, and you would begin to develop methods to reach your financial goals. You would be focused and would periodically check to see if your plan was working.

The Afrikan way adds the word "we" to the process. What if there was the existence of a group of Afrikans, who trusted each other, pooled their money, and invested those funds after studying and agreeing on what to invest. What would be your feelings about such a group? What if that same group doubled their pooled money every five years? What has been described is called an investment club. Ownership in stock gives one part ownership of the company. Investment clubs are, in fact, business owners. As mentioned, ownership has the greatest risk and, more importantly, the greatest reward in the United States system. Most rich people are rich not by having money in the bank but by having money in the stock market.

Though few investment clubs exist in Afrikan communities, there are some. They usually have ten to fifteen members, who are usually family and/or friends. Most clubs meet once a month. Most have monthly dues that range from twenty to one hundred dollars. Many clubs specialize in growth stocks, but some own land, bonds, and mutual funds. Most importantly, most of these clubs double their money every five to seven years. That is equal to receiving ten to fifteen percent per year on invested money.

What if each Afrikan family had an investment club? What if there were local councils of Afrikan investment clubs? What if these councils had a plan? What business would be safe from takeover by the Afrikan community? With an estimated 400 billion dollars of money to spend in the Afrikan community, what would happen if five percent was invested per year? Five percent amount to twenty billion dollars, making nearly half the businesses in the United States vulnerable to an Afrikan community takeover. This vulnerability is the main reason economics is not taught correctly in schools. The vulnerability of American business relates to the need to keep Afrikans confused about money and happy as consumers.

Economics is a vital part of human relations. Economics decides who we love, who we marry, where we live, what we wear and when and how we die. Something as important as economics requires continued and in-depth study. In order to revitalize the Afrikan community within the United States, it will take a clearer and more focused effort using Afrikan collective economic principles. Building a new economic reality must be paired with new methods of seeing ourselves, our brothers, and our sisters.

Since economics is such a vital part of living, a Rites of Passage program must teach economics. Trainers and trainees need to be exposed not only to the capitalist models and methods but also to the collective nature of Afrikan economics. They must further be exposed to the need for collective economics and the potential for power in collective economics. Nothing binds a family or a community together as much as economic self-interest. The key to Afrikan people in America thriving economically is using our collective economic resources in a meaningful and powerful manner.

Materials needed:	Same as previous Units
Didactic:	Teaching about indebtedness as a method of control Teaching about stocks and bonds Pooling resources with others to achieve a common goal The pyramid structure of Economics
Experiential:	Exercise in buying and selling stock
Media:	*George Washington Carver* Film on setting up an investment club Hapi Film
Biography:	Five Star International (an investment club) Reggie Lewis

Literature:	*The Charge* by Listervelt Middleton Read this poem very carefully. What is the poet saying to young people? What is the charge given? Is there a challenge? What is a "charge"? What does he say about today's values for Afrikan youth? Analyze each line.
Field Trip:	Visit brokerage house or an investment banker
Expected Outcome:	Trainee will get better understanding of Economics, the power of money, and money management in this system. Trainee will understand cooperative economics.

Didactic

The study of Economics is usually reserved until late high school or college. Students who are not bound for college seldom take the course. Yet, economics is one of the most important courses taught in school and is often the most boring. Coupled with religious teachings that discourage the accumulation of personal wealth, Afrikan people in the United States function financially in a disastrous fashion. "The love of money is the root of all evil" is often quoted as the cause of problems in our society. In reality, the lack of money is more often the real cause of problems. The lack of money causes people to steal, sell drugs, have poor health, and poor diets. The lack of money is the root of most people being in jail. It causes people to be scorned and ridiculed. The lack of money provides for a poverty mentality and causes people to make wrong choices about money.

Making choices about money is the definition of Economics. The choice made in the Afrikan communities throughout this country is to spend. Thus, we are a community of consumers. Even our consumption is not done wisely. We spurn Black businesses in favor of all others, and our money does not circulate in our community but circulates well in the communities of others. Afrikan people experience high unemployment not because other people will not "give us" jobs but because we create few jobs of our own. Our money flows directly out of our community into the community of others. Other communities then continue to become wealthy off of the sweat and labor of African people. Nothing has changed regarding slavery except the methods. Slavery was and is an economic system and principle. The only thing that has changed is the methods.

Why make a people work for free as slaves when they turn all of their money earned over to you willingly? In slavery, the master is required to provide food, clothing, and shelter to the slave. In the present economic method, the slave pays the master and takes care of his own food, clothing, and shelter. Understanding how the economic system works and how to utilize it for you, your family, and the community good is the goal of this unit.

AUSA are not poor, at least not the vast majority. In fact, the United States would be a very poor country if Afrikan people were to quit spending at the record levels which are currently happening. What we spend money on is quite interesting. We buy from anybody other than Afrikan people, and we even have made outright racists rich. To create wealth in our community, we must buy and spend wisely at businesses that employ and are owned by Afrikan people. We also need to learn to invest and to save money. Why should you do this? The answers to that question may seem somewhat selfish until you look at the whole picture.

Afrikans spend more than 50 billion dollars annually above and beyond household and transportation needs. These are monies spent on things we want (and don't necessarily need). Fifty billion dollars is the combined costs of multiple state governments, especially in the southeast. Fifty billion dollars employs nearly one million people and provides all services rendered by these states. Seventy percent of all Afrikans in America live in these states. The creation of businesses and, more important, jobs for the masses of Afrikan people is within our reach.

Most Afrikans will eventually retire. The way we spend, Afrikans will be forced to live off of Social Security and whatever pension their former company provides. This will probably not be enough for them to live on. It is estimated that if you are in your teens in the 1990s, you will need Social Security, your pension, and more than two million dollars in savings to live comfortably in the future. Accumulating that kind of money demands an understanding of economics beyond the current levels and strategies to legitimately reach that goal. Your very existence in old age depends upon it.

Working for money is good, but we cannot accumulate wealth by work alone. We must have a strategy. However, the strategy must be fueled by knowledge of how the economic system works. This system is composed of three parts: owners, producers/distributors, and consumers. Owners make the most money, followed by producers/ distributors, and finally, consumers who make the least amount of money. Ninety-five percent of Afrikans comprise the consumer level of the economic pyramid. Yet, the combined incomes of the Afrikan consumer group are larger than the combined wealth of Canada. This leads to the economic strategy for Afrikan people.

In order to provide wealth for ourselves and our community, we need to pool resources. This can best be done by developing investment clubs and organizations. We must learn both how to work for money and how to make money work for us. How we learn is by studying what rich people do. Rich people get rich by investing and owning rather than by going to work every day. We should learn to live off ninety percent of what we earn working and invest or save the remaining ten percent. That ten percent equates to five billion dollars per year collectively or, in other words, enough money to buy IBM, CBS, NBC, and ABC. Think of the Afrikan community's economic, social, and political clout if we owned just those four companies.

It must be stressed that although it is important to build wealth for ourselves and our families, we must have a vision of what that wealth can do for Afrikan people worldwide.

Experiential

Exercise #1

Reading the stock market is important to investing. Stocks provide a greater return for the money than any other investment or savings for the past 150 years. Reading and understanding the market is surprisingly easy. Provide each trainee with a copy of the stock page labeled NYSE. The trainers should teach the trainees how to read this page. Remember owning stock in a company means ownership in that company.

Exercise #2

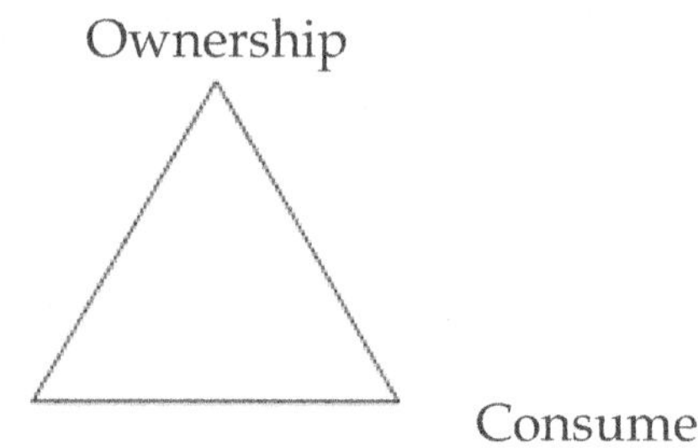

Divide the group in half. Each group is now an investment club. Give each group member a piece of paper with "$5000" written on it. Have each member of the group select one stock to spend $5000 on. Record the purchases on the chart below. Review the charts one week later to see what has happened.

Name of stock selected	Cost of one share	Number of shares purchased	Name of who will keep track of this stock	Amount spent on this stock

Media

The video George Washington Carver is a spiritually enlightening recounting of the life of an extremely important man. Through Carver's work for the community, he aided in the establishment of Tuskegee Institute. His was the spirit of working together for the good of his people. Question the trainees about how their goals will benefit the community and how they can assist in leading the community toward the path of economic security.

The National Association of Investment Clubs provides an excellent video on starting an investment club. These clubs throughout the United States own parts of companies and are considered a collective powerhouse. Less than one percent of Afrikan people belong to an investment club.

The film, Hapi, gives a history of economics starting from ancient Afrika to today.

Biographies

Five Star International Investment Club

Five Star International is an investment club of AUSA in Columbia, South Carolina. The club has averaged about ten members, from all walks of life and vocations, since its beginning in the early 1980s. Each member pays dues of twenty dollars a month. The members then decide on a stock to purchase with the dues.

Since its beginning, the members have contributed about $20,000 in dues. The total worth of the Investment Club is well over $50,000. Five Star has a long-term strategy for the club, and some members also have individual stock holdings modeled after the Club portfolio. Pooling money works.

Field Trip

Visit a brokerage house or an investment banker. Nearly every town has a large bank, and usually, someone at the bank can provide a tour and this kind of information. They can also tell you about other types of investments such as bonds, certificates of deposit, and money market accounts.

References and Suggested Reading for Unit Six

Anderson, Claud. *Black Labor, White Wealth: The Search for Power and Economic Justice*. Chevy Chase, MD: Powernomics Corporation of America, 1994

Boston, Kelvin. *Smart Money Moves for African American*, NY: A Perigee Book, Published by The Berkeley Publishing Group,1996

Chinweizu. *The West and the Rest of Us: White Predators, Black Slavers and the African Elite*, Lagos: Pero Press, 1987

Diop, Cheikh Anta. *Black Africa: The Economic and Cultural Basis for a Federated State*, Africa World Press Edition, Westport: Lawrence Hill and Company, 1987

Wilson, Amos. Blueprint for Black Power: A Moral, Political and Economic Imperative for the Twenty-First Century. Brooklyn: Afrikan World Infosystems, 2000

Unit Seven

"Ebonically Speaking"

Communication Skills, Art and Aesthetic

"In my music, my plays, my films, I want to carry always this central idea: to be Afrikan. Multitudes of men have died for less worthy ideals; it is even more eminently worth living for."

-Paul Robeson

The prominent psychologist, Dr. Robert Williams coined the word Ebonics by combining the words ebony and phonics. The word "ebony" means "Black", and the word "phonics" means "sounds." When put together, these words mean "Black sounds." Dr. Williams tried to give linguistic legitimacy to how Afrikans in America express themselves through these "Black sounds." Language is the vehicle by which culture is imparted. Imagine the horribly degrading and humiliating conditions that Afrikans had to endure during the Middle Passage. It is not only amazing that we survived but that we were simultaneously able to develop a way of imparting information that would allow us to have intergenerational conversations.

The Middle Passage and subsequent enslavement of Afrikan people in the Americas continent (the Maafa) is one of the cruelest crimes ever committed against humanity in the history of the world. As mentioned in previous chapters, Afrikan people pulled upon our ancestors' strength and the culture they developed in Afrika to survive this horrific period in our history. The segment of our culture that we will focus on in this chapter is "Communication."

What are some of the core elements of how we communicate that allowed us to develop a unique and effective way of imparting information from one generation to the next? Are these elements still in use today? If so, then how and in what ways do they manifest themselves? Answering these and other questions can and will give us some insight into what we need to do to help develop our youth into the kind of adults who will serve their community and stop being participants in the destruction of their community.

There are many forms of communication. Effective communication can be verbal through language and other sounds and can also be non-verbal through cultural arts. One definition of art is creating and doing things that have form and beauty. This definition would include painting, sculpture, architecture, music, literature, drama, dance, entertainment, sports, cosmetics, poetry, and fashion.

The word "aesthetics" comes from the Greek word "aisthetikos," which means "perceived by feeling." For our use, aesthetics will be defined as the theory of fine art and how people respond to it. In short, the information passed on through art allows people to respond in positive and negative ways.

There is a very basic core component that all cultures use as the foundation of their art expression. This core component has to do with how groups of people perceive their position in the world. Every culture has a view of the world that places itself at the center. This view of the world is the foundation of all art forms.

According to anthropologists, a worldview is that aspect of culture which functions to replace presented disorder with perceived order. This order supplies its members with definitions of reality, which helps them make sense of their surroundings and experiences. Dr. Wade Nobles of San Francisco State University has told us that this deep structure of reality has a most profound influence on the shape of a culture and the thought patterns of its members.

In the deep structure of reality for people of Afrikan ancestry, there are some very basic influences. Most of these influences have to do with our relationship with the Creator (Supreme Being). This relationship, being one of reverence, allows us as a people to see God's creations as gifts. Out of this reality comes the idea that being in harmony with God's creations will allow us to be in harmony with the Creator. When we gaze into the sky and notice the Creator's greatest gift, the sun, we don't want to subdue or control it but to live in harmony with it. Developing harmonious relationships with the Creator's manifestations like the cosmos, nature, other humans, those who have passed through this life before us (ancestor veneration), and those yet to come will ultimately lead us on a quest for human perfectibility.

Dr. Marimba Ani is a social scientist and anthropologist and is a former professor of Black Studies at Hunter College, City University of New York. In her seminal work, *Yurugu,* she gives us some insight into the deep structure of realities that influence all cultures. Utilizing Afrikan language forms to describe and explain the kinds of processes and mechanisms found in culture, Dr. Ani uses Ki-Swahili terms to define these cultural modalities. Dr. Ani states, *"The Asili is the logos of a culture, within which its various aspects cohere. It is the developmental germ/seed of a culture." She goes on to say that "it is the cultural essence, the ideological core, the matrix of a cultural entity which must be identified in order to make sense of the collective creations of its members. Utamawazo is culturally structured thought. It is the way in which cognition is determined by the cultural asili. It is the way in which the thought of the members of a culture must be patterned if the asili is to be fulfilled. Utamaroho is the vital force of a culture set in motion by the asili. It is the trust or energy source of a culture; that which gives it its emotional tone and motivates the collective behavior of its members."*

The utamawazo and the utamaroho emerge from the asili. They should not be thought of as separate and apart from the asili but as manifestations of the asili. Another way of looking at this is that the asili is a seed with the DNA genetic makeup of the culture. This cultural DNA manifests itself in the form of thought (utamawazo) and behavior (utamaroho). So, the way we think and behave as a cultural collective can be traced to our cultural DNA.

Let us, for a moment, imagine an apple seed. Inside of an apple seed is all of the genetic information necessary for this apple seed to produce a tree that would bear apples. For the purpose of this analysis, we will call this genetic information "apple DNA." When an apple seed filled with its apple DNA is cultivated and planted under the optimal environmental conditions for maximum growth, the expectation is to see a tree bearing apples based on the genetic information locked in the seed. We, the planter, can never see this genetic information with our naked eye. We can assume, however, from past experience (History) and tradition (Culture) handed down through the ages that a tree with apples will appear. In fact, one would be shocked and amazed if anything other than the seed you planted started to grow.

When Dr. Ani speaks of the asili (seed) of any culture, she is saying that locked in the respective cultures of different groups of people is their cultural DNA. When cultivated and put under optimal conditions for growth, the tree that emerges has two recognizable limbs: cultural thought (utamawazo) and cultural behavior (utamaroho). If one knows what the cultural DNA locked in the asili is, then one knows the type of fruit (human) the tree will produce. The behavior (utamaroho) and thought (utamawazo) can never be more than what is locked in the asili. You should not expect anything different or more than what that asili can produce. If you want to know why Afrikans do what they do, look at their cultural DNA (asili). If you wonder why people of European descent think (utamawazo) and behave (utamaroho) a certain way, look at their asili (cultural DNA). People cannot and will not act or operate any different than what is in their respective asili. Yes, we are all humans, but different groups of people have different cultural values and qualities. Different, not superior or inferior; different, not better or worse.

At the core of the Afrikan cultural asili is "Black Sound," which we will call "sacred rhythm." Sacred rhythm is the combining of spirituality and rhythm. This is the essence of life. All matter comes into existence through sacred rhythmic motion. Traditionally, Afrikan people have always moved to the spiritual forces in their psyches. What we call spirit is sacred rhythm. It binds us as a people. Intuitively, people of Afrikan descent understand that if one wants to reach the goal of human perfectibility by becoming one with the Creator, then it is essentially to become harmonious with the sacred rhythm of life. At the core of this intuitive understanding is that we are spiritual beings having a human encounter, not human beings having a spiritual encounter.

Dr. William Gunn, a former professor at Benedict College in Columbia, S.C., sheds some light on the subject of rhythm and spirituality in an essay he wrote for the Afrikan American Resource Institute of South Carolina (AARI-SC) titled "African Spirituality and Rhythmic Movement." In this article, he states that, *"The ancient Egyptians (or Kamites or Kamieu as they called themselves – meaning the Black people of the Black land) realized thousands of years ago that the activity of the celestial bodies in the cosmos provided the key to understanding rhythmic spirituality. They observed that the sun rotated around the celestial bodies in perfect rhythm; and that the stars were in perfect harmony with each other. They also noticed that as the sun rotated through the solar system, it exerted a power on earth that ultimately had an effect on the destinies of nations and individuals."* Afrikan people often express this idea of sacred rhythm through their cultural art forms, such as their sacred dance and music. Sacred music and dance (sacred rhythm) were performed at harvest time, funerals, and weddings. Each dance movement and song had its own meaning and was used to communicate with the Creator and with each other.

In 1972, Lee Warren published a book called *The Dance of Africa,* where he pointed out that: *"Among the exciting sights and sounds of Black Africans is not only their dance but the way it is performed. Woven throughout the pattern of African life, dancing for Afrikans is more than the recreation it is for Westerners. With the music, which is inseparable from it, dancing is part of living itself. The response of the body to expressions of love, joy, grief, and despair all to the accompaniment of music, songs, and drumming is the heritage of the African. To see an African dance is to witness his cultural past and present. Africans use their bodies to reflect their emotions, their hopes, and their religion. The head moves in one rhythm, the shoulders in another, the arms in still a third, the feet in still another. Their dance is text in motion, linked to the music of the drums, instruments, and voices."*

The transatlantic slave trade and colonialism did not remove the strong sacred rhythmic, and very spiritual relationship with the God of the universe. In fact, Afrikans were able to create new cultural art forms that allowed the asili to be fulfilled. While in the fields as slaves, Afrikans moved their bodies and created songs. These songs expressed their feelings of distress, grief, and their faith in God to get them through. These sacred rhythms, songs, and dances unified the Afrikans who came from different ethnic groups. They created the "ring shouts" when dancing in a circle which shows a realization of the past, present, and future being one.

This new unifying sacred rhythm that slavery produced set in motion the emergence of what we now call the Black Church. The Black Church emerged as the center where Afrikans could go to express their fears, hopes, frustrations, anger, and love. The focal point of this new unifying sacred rhythm was an old traditional cultural thought (utamawazo) known as "call" and cultural behavior (utamaroho) known as "response." This social, linguistic way of communicating allowed the speaker (preachers) to interact with the audience.

When in the midst of an audience of people of Afrikan descent, the speaker expects to hear responses of "amen" or "right-on brother." In fact, if the speaker (preacher) does not receive any response, he/she knows to change the nature of the speech. This "call and response" model was directly related to the "call and response" music of Afrika. This preaching/speaking and singing style offered a most powerful way for African people to move the spiritual forces within them and create sacred rhythmic body movement, allowing the participator to be harmonious with the Creator.

When emancipation came, new unanswered questions arose that turned into problems for some of us. These new social, economic, and political problems stemmed from the fact that we did not know how we would sustain ourselves now that we no longer had "old massa" to rely on for our sustenance. This new pressure produced new sacred rhythms, which the church could not answer. Out of this reality came a series of music and dance in which we were trying to find new ways to fulfill our cultural DNA (asili). Jazz and the Blues were the answer to some of the new realities in which we found ourselves. Although these were new sacred rhythms, they were largely developed through the experiences of Afrikans in America and still frequently used the "call and response" style. Throughout our Maafa in this country, we have always been able to respond to the pressure put upon our cultural DNA with new expressions of cultural thought and behavior that allowed Afrikan people to remain one with the Creator. The Afrikans' ability to create new art forms which kept us in harmony with God has been most powerful and influenced the way we were able to survive the hardship of the Maafa.

Music and dance have been profoundly integral parts of the way we communicate our hopes, fears, and frustrations. In fact, the only true American art forms were created by people of Afrikan descent. To know what influenced our people in this country, follow the music, dance, and sacred rhythm through the 500 years we have been on this continent, from the work songs, "ring shouts," and singing of "Go Down Moses" to the singing of the sacred rhythm, e.g., "Precious Lord;" from Billie Holliday who told us about "Strange Fruit" to John Coltrane who said there is a "Love Supreme"; from Aretha Franklin who said what we want is a little "Respect" to the Temptations who said in "Message to the Black Man," *"No matter how hard you try you can't stop me now."* Then Marvin Gaye came along and asked the question, "What's going on?" and Gil Scott-Heron answered with a sacred rhythm that said, "The Revolution will not be Televised." We have tried to communicate to the world through our sacred rhythm our past, present, and future.

Even in athletics, our sacred rhythm manifested itself. There is no doubt that Dr. Neismith did not have the Black athlete in mind when he invented basketball. The object of basketball is to take a round ball and put it in a basket. Eventually, a hole was cut into the bottom of the basket so the ball would drop through and, it would be a lot easier to retrieve the ball. Then the Black athlete comes along and in satisfying his cultural asili of sacred rhythm and motion, decided that putting the ball between his legs and jumping in the air while turning 360 degrees and then dunking the ball behind his head was infinitely more pleasing than just shooting the ball in the basket. This sacred rhythmic motion is found in any sport that the Black athletes participate in. Whether it's the fluid motion of Barry Sanders or the poetry-in-motion of Muhammad Ali, this sacred rhythm is at the center of their humanness.

The clothing that we wear is also a method of communication. This not only includes what we wear, but how we wear it. What messages are boys communicating when they wear their pants so low that the split between the buttocks can be easily seen? What messages are girls communicating when they wear dresses or skirts so short and tight that they can hardly walk or sit comfortably? What messages are being conveyed when shoelaces are left untied? No men or women who have power in any culture dress in this manner. When we gather together in our Afrikan organizations and wear European clothing, what message are we giving our children? This indirect, nonverbal form of communication is readily picked up by our children and can have a profound effect on what they view as important and what personal standards to choose. This information causes our youth to, too frequently, place too high a value on fashion. In this situation, it becomes easier to understand why many children would beg, borrow, or steal in order to wear clothing that makes them feel important.

It is unfortunate when we call our native clothing "costumes" and relegate the wearing of them to "dress down days" at work or at church. Our children should see adults wearing our native clothing proudly and frequently in many different settings. This will reinforce a positive self-image and help them in choosing appropriate things to value.

There is an old saying that "Beauty is in the eye of the beholder." In art and aesthetics, the beholder is the culture. One's culture determines what beauty is and what is pleasing to the eye. All too often, Afrikans allow other cultures to define beauty for them. This is very obviously seen in our appearances. We often "fry, dye, and barbecue" (use hot combs, artificial coloring, and chemical straighteners) our hair. We change our facial features (when we can afford to) in order to look like non-Afrikans. We frequently get contact lenses that make our eyes lighter in color. We spend billions of dollars in the "ugly industry," also known as the cosmetics and hair care industries. Although Afrikans supposedly make up only 12% of the population of the United States, we spend approximately 40% of all the sales in the cosmetics industry. This amounts to more than 40 billion dollars yearly. We have allowed others to define our beauty based on their standards. In order for us to call the place where we go to "look good" a "beauty parlor," ugly has to walk in. Even then, the "beautician" has to protect himself or herself from the beauty-inducing chemicals by wearing protective garments such as gloves and goggles. The customer gets directly exposed to these chemicals in the name of "beauty," however. Consider, if the "beauticians" have to protect themselves from the chemicals that are being applied directly to the customer, what are the chemicals doing to the customer?

Women and men have attempted to enhance their appearances for untold thousands of years, and there is nothing wrong with this. It seems sick, however, to expose oneself to potential harm to look like someone else. We should remain true to our sacred rhythm and see fashion and cosmetics as more than the wearing of clothes and getting a new "do." It would seem that our appearances should reflect and communicate our culture.

Ebonics is a way of communicating for Afrikan people outside of Afrika. Since we were forcibly taken from Afrika, we weren't fortunate enough to have someone patiently teach us the language of our captors. In fact, Ebonics is widely spoken. The words depend on the language of the captor/kidnapper/colonizer, but the sentence structure is definitely Afrikan. As an example, Ebonics spoken in America uses mostly English words. Ebonics spoken in Haiti uses mostly French words. Ebonics spoken in Puerto Rico uses mostly Spanish words, and Ebonics spoken in Brazil uses Portuguese words. The sentence structure and other elements of speech are Afrikan in origin despite the words used. The oppressor did not bother to formally teach his language to the people he was oppressing. Therefore, as the oppressed learned words, they used them in the context of their own Afrikan languages.

In America, many Afrikans are frustrated by the inadequacy of American English to completely express their emotions. As a result, there are expressions used in the Afrikan community that express the ideas that American English cannot "handle." These expressions, when used, usually have a rhythm and vocal inflection that allows the speaker to elicit emotions from the listener that touches his/her inner being (sacred rhythm).

As an example, Ebonics has five present tenses:

1. He runnin' (He is running.)
2. He be runnin' ("He is currently running" or depending on emphasis, "He is really running well.")
3. He be steady runnin' (He is running in an intensively sustained manner.)
4. He been runnin' (He has been running for a while.)
5. He done been runnin' (He has been running for a long time and is still running.)

These tenses are the same as in most Bantu languages of Afrika. In fact, in January 1997, the Linguistic Society of America, at its annual meeting, unanimously approved a resolution describing Ebonics as "systematic and rule-governed like all natural speech varieties."

The arguments given by our so-called "leaders" against Ebonics are so ridiculous as to be scary. These arguments (frequently made in Ebonics) expose the person speaking as someone who doesn't listen or understand well, as someone who is stupid, or as someone who is doing the bidding of others. No one in Oakland wanted to teach children Ebonics (they already spoke it). They wanted to expose teachers to the rules of Ebonics so they could more effectively teach Ebonics-speaking children Standard American English without damaging their psyches.

Language is a major vehicle by which culture is imparted. We must recognize and respect our culture and withstand efforts by others to make us ashamed of who we are.

Hip Hop or Rap music is a musical medium that has captured the imagination of our youth. Rap must be seen as a cultural continuum of communicative expression through our sacred rhythm. Rap is the bringing together of our ancestors' sacred rhythms through previously recorded music as part of the background and how we verbally communicate through rhyming. From Curtis Blow, who said: "These are the Breaks" to Public Enemy, who told us to: "Fight the Powers That Be," this new art form maintained the cultural integrity that was always present in our music.

Now that we have allowed those who do not have our best interest as a people at heart to be the producers and distributors of our sacred rhythm, it has created a generation of young adults who think gang banging and calling sisters bitches and whores, is a way of life. The problem is not with the art form or culture of Rap music (Hip Hop), it is in the message that is allowed to permeate the radio airways. This is made more serious when we consider that these are the images and messages shown overseas to Afrika youth (and other places) who have been convinced to idolize all things American. Remember, nothing just happens; obviously, the kind of behaviors that have taken over the culture is by design.

The Afrikans who were forcibly brought to America brought their own desires, beliefs, rituals, and customs with them. They were brought to a place with a radically different culture and customs than those with which they were accustomed. They were faced with cruelty and intentional dehumanization, the like of which they had dared not imagine. They were placed in contact with people whose beliefs and philosophies were the antithesis of all their beliefs, and philosophies. They were placed in constant contact with a people who did not recognize God as the center of all that is. This encounter, for the Afrikans, was (and still is) profoundly traumatic.

The transformation from Afrikan to American had to happen over several generations. The first generation saw themselves as captives and not slaves. They had known freedom and longed for the day when they would again be free. Unfortunately, each subsequent generation began to lose some of the ability to identify with Afrika because enslavement was all they knew. Many of them became American Negroes and would (will) jump through hoops just as trained animals will. It is a matter of their socialization. That this Negro has continued to produce methods of communication, art, and aesthetics that adhered to his/her sacred rhythm is remarkable but obviously lies in their asili.

This unit is designed not to just give a historical view of how we communicate through our music, dance, and sacred rhythm; but to show how Afrikan people have lost their way on the road to human perfectibility. This unit is also designed to give the trainee what he/she will need to do to return to the right road. Somewhere along the path, we made a left turn when the sign on the road said, "The way to God's house is straight ahead through the Sacredness of your Rhythm." We must "Honor" and remain steadfast and unmovable in being "Loyal" to our sacred rhythm. We must also allow it to be of "Service" to us in our quest for human perfectibility.

There are many forms of communication that people use to interact with each other. Effective communication is not only verbal through the use of language, but it is also and mostly nonverbal through cultural art forms. In this Unit, the participant will be provided with an understanding of Art and Aesthetics. The historical, philosophical, and cultural significance of Art and how it is used as a form of communication will be explored.

Materials needed:	Same as previous Units
Didactic:	Discussion of beauty. Define art and aesthetics. What does art do for one's culture? Importance of art in ancient Afrikan history. How is art a form of communication? Discussion of use and importance of affect, effect, body language, and sign language. Effective verbal communication, including discussion of the differences between Ebonics and slang.
Experiential:	Revisit ancient Kemetic art through the statues Five square game Communication through music, including rap
Media:	Wattstax Sign Language video
Field Trip:	Museum of art Recording studio Discussion with an actor School for the deaf

Biography: Larry Lebby
Leo Twiggs
Romare Bearden
Tom Feelings
Seitu Amenwahsu
Augusta Savage
Edmonia Lewis
Jacob Lawrence
Listervelt Middleton

Literature: *Mother to Son* by Langston Hughes
The Bluest Eye by Toni Morrison

Expected Outcome: The participants will develop an appreciation for Art. They will understand the meaning of Aesthetics, its significance in all cultures, how it is manipulated and how it is used as a form of communication.

Didactic

There is an old saying that "Beauty is in the eye of the beholder." In the area of Art and Aesthetics, the beholder is the culture. One's culture determines what beauty is and what is pleasing to the eye. All too often, the Afrikan American community allows other cultures to define beauty for them. This is very obviously seen in our appearances. To "look good," we often "fry, dye, and barbecue" (place hot combs and chemicals) in our hair and change our facial features to fit definitions of beauty given to us by others who don't look like us. Each culture uses art as a way to communicate and express to the world how they see themselves and how they feel about themselves.

In this Unit, the trainee will learn what beauty is, according to the Afrikan and Afrikan American standard of beauty. An overhead projector (or slide projector) may be used to show pictures of ancient and contemporary Afrika. The features of the Afrikans should be pointed out, and the following questions asked:

1) Why were the features important enough to be included in these monuments?
2) Do we still value the features of our Ancestors? Why or why not?

Music is also an art form. The trainer will discuss the importance that music has always played in the life of Afrikans. The trainer should be familiar with the different types of music found in our communities (e.g., blues, gospel, rhythm and blues, jazz, rap, reggae, drumming, continental Afrikan etc.) and should be familiar with music from different eras.

The clothing that we wear is also an expression of ourselves (this includes what we wear and how we wear it).

The goal of this lecture is to help the trainee understand that there are many forms of communication. We as a people are making statements to the world and to each other through the way that we dress, through our music, and through our art. These forms of communication (verbal and nonverbal) help people of other cultures to know you and helps them to decide how they should treat you. If they believe that you have no respect for yourself, then they will not have any respect for you and will treat you accordingly.

Ebonics is a way of communicating that Afrikan people outside of Afrika have used since they were forcibly taken away from Afrika. It is an Afrikan language, but the words depend on the language of the kidnapper/colonizer. Still, the morphology, syntax and other parts of the language are West

Afrikan. Ebonics is appropriate to be spoken at home and in private with friends. It is NOT appropriate to be spoken at work, at interviews or other formal/semi-formal public places. Standard American English must be learned.

Experiential

Broken Squares

Broken squares is an exercise in working together. Even under the best of conditions, people have great difficulty working on joint tasks. This exercise allows a group to explore the frustrations and behaviors associated with working in groups.

HOW THE EXERCISE WORKS

1) The facilitator does a short lecture on working together.
2) The facilitator picks five people to be in the group to perform the tasks.
3) The facilitator picks two people to be observers. The observers should have a pencil and pad to record what they observe.

4) NOTE: If you have an audience of more than seven, you may want to have more than one group doing this exercise.

5) Each group participant should be seated around one table and given an envelope containing pieces of squares. They are requested not to open the envelopes until the instructions are given and the facilitator says GO.

INSTRUCTIONS: The task is complete when all five have a square in front of them.

1) When the envelopes are open, there can be no talking.
2) The group is to construct 5 five-inch by five-inch squares.
3) The parts of the squares are mixed up, so no one can make a square from the contents of his or her envelop.
4) Observers are to watch for talking because there is no talking at all during this exercise.
5) Make sure each person who has an envelope rechecks to make sure they have taken out all pieces.
6) Any person with an envelope can give a piece of his or her square away, but no one can take a piece from another person or ask that a piece be given.

Special note to the facilitator: a diagram of the squares is attached. Each square should be five inches by five inches. Mix the parts up and put them in envelopes. Unless the five squares are put together like in the diagram, the group will only be able to construct three or four squares. It normally takes between 15 to 30 minutes to complete this task. The debriefing is the most important part.

DEBRIEFING

The facilitator leads the discussion. The conversation should revolve around the visual observations of the observers and the feelings of the group members.

Some will express frustration.
Some will give up.
Some will take over.
Some will withdraw from the group.
Some will gang up on those not participating.

Some will violate the rules.
Some will want to violate the rules.
Some will be too frustrated to talk.

If the conversation is slow, which is not unusual for teenage groups, you may want to spark the conversation with some of the above questions like:

Was anyone frustrated?
Observers, did everyone participate equally?

(The next page is a diagram of 5 squares)

DIRECTIONS FOR MAKING A SET OF BROKEN SQUARES

A set consists of five envelopes containing pieces of cardboard cut into different patterns which, when properly arranged, will form five squares of equal size. One set should be provided for each group of five persons.

To prepare a set, cut out five cardboard squares, each exactly 6″ × 6″. Place the squares in a row and mark them as below, penciling the letters lightly so they can be erased.

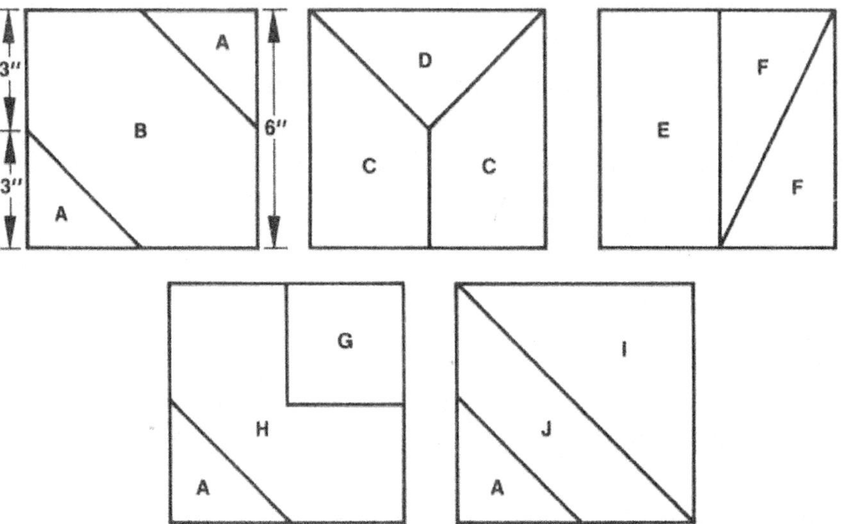

The lines should be so drawn that, when the pieces are cut out, those marked A will be exactly the same size, all pieces marked C the same size, etc. Several combinations are possible that will form one or two squares, but only one combination will form all five squares, each 6″×6″. After drawing the lines on the squares and labeling the sections with letters, cut each square along the lines into smaller pieces to make the parts of the puzzle.

Label the five envelopes 1, 2, 3, 4, and 5. Distribute the cardboard pieces into the five envelopes as follows: envelope 1 has pieces I, H, E; 2 has A, A, A, C; 3 has A, J; 4 has D, F; and 5 has G, B, F, C.

Erase the penciled letter from each piece and write, instead, the number of the envelope it is in. This makes it easy to return the pieces to the proper envelope, for subsequent use, after a group has completed the task.

Each set may be made from a different color of cardboard.

References and Suggested Reading for Unit Seven

Blackshire-Belay, Carol Aisha (1996): The Location of Ebonics Within the Framework of the Africological Paradigm, *Journal of Black Studies*, 27 (1): 5-23.

Browder, Anthony T. *From the Browder File: 22 Essays on the African American Experience*, Washington: The Institute of Karmic Guidance, 1989

Browder, Anthony T. *From the Browder File, Volume II: Survival Strategies for Africans in America: 13 Steps to Freedom*, Washington: The Institute of Karmic Guidance, 1996

Cohen, Jeff and Norman Solomon (1995): *Through the Media Looking Glass: Decoding Bias and Blather in the News*, Monroe, ME: Common Courage Press, 1995

Dates, Janette L. and William Barlow (editors) (1993): *Split Image: African Americans in the Mass Media*, Washington, D.C.: Howard University Press, 1993

Hilliard, Asa G., III (1983): Psychological Factors Associated with Language in the Education of the African-American Child, *Journal of Negro Education* 52 (1): 24-34.

McGraw, Patricia Washington. The Truth About Ebonics: The Historically Sound Language System Spoken by Most African Americans: A Linguist Speaks, *Arkansas State Press*, Thursday, January 30, 1997

Parenti, Michael. *Inventing Reality: The Politics of the News Media*, NY: St. Martin's Press, 1993

Smith, Ernie A. (1978): The Historical Development of Ebonics, *Western Journal of Black Studies* 2(3): 202-207.

Turner, Patricia A. *Ceramic Uncles and Celluloid Mammies: Black Images and Their Influence on Culture*, NY: Anchor Books, 1994

Unit Eight

"To Be Healthy or Not to Be"

Health, Hygiene, and Science

"The aim of African education for the mind could not be separated from education for the body. The body was seen as a divine temple, having a spirit. As a result, the education for mind and body was also linked to education for the spirit."

-Asa G. Hilliard, III

Afrikans have traditionally been the cleanest people in the world. Even Homer in *The Iliad* commented on the cleanliness of "the blameless Ethiopians" (note that at that time, the word "Ethiopian" was applied to all people that we now call Afrikan or Black). In that same book, Homer also discussed the fact that Afrikans were the world leaders in medical treatment and technology at that time and, as a result of this health care superiority, were "...the healthiest of all men."

Unfortunately, since that time, there has been a tragic and profound reversal of that observation. The health of Afrikans in America and, indeed, Afrikan people all over the world is deteriorating despite technical advances in medical sciences. Much of this is related to a lack of information as well as access. If Afrikan people had the information, the problem of access could be addressed and solved much more easily.

A major part of any Rites of Passage program MUST include health and hygiene. By nature, many (if not most) young people are adventurous and frequently do not adequately consider the consequences of their actions. The realities of today's world are so stark that this type of behavior becomes quite dangerous.

There are several areas in which this general topic can be explored. It can be used as a unit or introduced early on and reinforced at regular intervals during the training period. We have separated the most worrisome areas into these categories: Mental Health, Hygiene, Human Sexuality, Sexually Transmitted Diseases, Drug use, Common illnesses of African People, Parenting and Child Care, and Dietary Choices Nutrition. There is a definite interrelationship among all these areas, and this fact has to be stressed.

Throughout the process, there are historical individuals that the trainee is asked to find out about. These historical figures add to their comprehension of the topic. Some of these historical figures are: Imhotep, Peseshet, Hesy-Ra, Sekh-Met, Charles Drew, Daniel Hale Williams, James Derham, James McCune Smith, William Wells Brown, Rebecca Lee, Montague W. Cobb, Rebecca J. Cole, Susan Smith McKinney Steward, and Martin Delany (to name a few).

Mental Health

The process of creating slaves from kidnapped Afrikans included, in great part, creating mental illness in those Afrikans. This process has been termed our "Maafa." Subsequently, beings were created that placed the values, well-being, worldview, and culture of their enslavers and oppressors above their own. Some individuals continue to demonstrate this mental illness, even today. Several Afrikan American (Ausa) Psychologists have studied this matter closely and have defined and classified these illnesses. We'd like to recommend the book by Dr. Kobi Kambon (aka Joseph Baldwin), *The African Personality in America: An African-Centered Framework,* be studied closely in order to know and understand what is normal and healthy.

Dr. Na'im Akbar has proposed four categories of mental illness:

1. The Alien-Self Disorders include Afrikans who have rejected their Afrikanness. They see themselves and others as having worth only according to their material possessions and accumulations. They deny the existence of white supremacy and oppression. In effect, they live in a dream world. This disorder is becoming epidemic among the so-called middle-class and professional Ausa people. People with this disorder don't really feel comfortable with themselves and become neurotic and frequently seek psychiatric and psychological help.

2. The Anti-Self Disorders include all the descriptions of the Alien-Self Disorders plus covert and overt hostility towards everything and everyone Afrikan, including themselves and their families. People with this disorder actually feel quite comfortable identifying with the oppressors and are the "sell-outs" among the Ausa who will betray their parents or siblings in order to get ahead.

3. Self-Destructive Disorders include those individuals who are "burned out" and overwhelmed from their attempts to survive. They have adopted meanness as their way of surviving white supremacy. People with this disorder become the criminals, substance abusers, and psychotics in our communities. People with this disorder have either refused to accept or have not had the opportunity to develop the alien self-identity.

4. Organic Disorders, according to Akbar, "... includes the severely mentally defective, organic brain disorders and most of the commonly recognized forms of schizophrenia." This group also includes senility. He feels that, in many cases, these may be the result of abnormal psychosocial conditions in society. He cites

such factors as poor nutrition, effects of drugs that may bypass one or two generations, and environmental toxins as causing these problems.

Dr. Daudi Ajani ya Azibo has studied the work of many Ausa psychologists and psychiatrists and has attempted to combine them into a logical order. He uses the work of such noted scholars as Dr. Kobi Kambon, Dr. Wade W. Nobles, Dr. Na'im Akbar, Dr. Frances Cress Welsing, Dr. Bobby Wright, Dr. Franz Fanon, Dr. George G. Jackson, Dr. Robert L. Williams, and many more to formulate his compendium. A brief outline of Dr. Azibo's work follows:

1. Psychological misorientation is the basic Afrikan personality disorder and consists of operating without an Afrikan Centered belief system. Azobo equates it to "genetic blackness minus psychological blackness." This problem is present whenever alien concepts dominate the conscious and subconscious minds, and he uses psychological Europeanism and psychological Arabism as an example.

2. Menticide is defined as a deliberate and systematic destruction of the minds of individuals or groups of individuals. Azibo discusses two types of menticide:
    a. Alienating menticide alienates the Afrikan from her/himself by attacking psychological blackness.
    b. Peripheral menticide creates disorganization of the peripheral part of the personality by creating/enabling the acquisition of a peripheral personality disorder.

3. Black personality disorders are always a function of menticide.

a. Materialistic depression occurs when material goods or the lack of material good serves as criteria for judging self and others. He cites as an example the observation of a person in a low-income job living in modest surroundings buying an expensive car.
b. Personality identity conflict has several manifestations.
    i. Individualism is the opposite of the Afrikan principles of collective responsibility and survival of the tribe.
    ii. Sexual misorientation, such as homosexuality and bisexuality that is non-genetically caused. This category also includes sexual perversions such as sex obsession which seems to propagate itself through generations.

4. WEUSI anxiety occurs when the above problems occur and are accompanied by obvious anxiety. WEUSI is a Swahili word meaning "black". WEUSI anxiety occurs when there is an internal conflict between being a strong black woman or man or being a European/American acting person.

5. Reactionary disorders are abnormal responses to oppression that indicate that coping mechanisms have broken down. Psychological brainwashing is a process used to purge a thought or ideology from a person's mind in order to control their thinking and actions. It causes Afrikans to argue and fight in defense of non-Afrikan control of their lives.
    a. Psychological burnout occurs at the point at which an individual involved in the struggle for survival and liberation is overwhelmed. This

person may become fatigued and even disillusioned.

b. Oppression violence reactions are violent acts that are not planned and may be directed at Afrikans as well as non-Afrikans. Their root causes are racism and oppression. These reactions occur more frequently in males because of the faulty definitions of Black manhood.

6. Self-Destructive Disorders are as explained by Akbar.

7. Organic Disorders are as explained by Akbar.

8. Theological misorientation occurs when an individual practice, believes in and has allegiance to a theology or religion-based ideology that is not consistent with Afrikan social theory, cosmology or history. It occurs whenever we do not only glorify non-Afrikan belief systems but also to turn us further against ourselves. Theological misorientation has one subcategory.
   a. Theological alienation is the revulsion towards the practice of even a non-Afrikan manner. This results in the destruction of the manifesting of Afrikan spirituality.

Dr. Samella Abdullah lists over-identification with the oppressor, feelings of estrangement from others; inability to see self in the future; lack of knowledge about history, culture, worldview, religion, self; poor self-image (requiring chemicals or other methods to create looks that conform to the "European Norm"); unrewarding interpersonal relationships; and practice of self-destructive behaviors as symptoms of "Post-Traumatic Stress Disorder in Afrikans."

Suicide in Ausa teenagers is one particularly distressing manifestation of mental illness in our community. The rate of suicide for all Afrikans (except Afrikan women) has increased significantly since the 1950s but has increased most in Afrikan teenagers. According to the Center for Disease Control in Atlanta, the rate of Afrikan teenage suicide has more than doubled from 1980 to 1995.

The emergence of youth cultures that take the place of strong family centered relationships is another example of our mental illness. We have adopted an alien definition of family, which is simply not working for us consistently at any socioeconomic level. The gang culture is one of these youth cultures in which gang relationships actually take precedence over family relationships. They also formalize many of the Self-Destructive Behaviors and make them a normal part of that culture.

It is our profound and sincere belief that Afrikan Centered Rites of Passage Programs will significantly reduce mental illness in our community. We strongly believe that the emphasis on Identity, Purpose, and Direction in Rites of Passage Programs will prevent and cure the overwhelming majority of mental illnesses in our community.

Human Sexuality

Most young people know, generally, where babies come from. Most, however, don't know the details of sexual functioning. While Rites of Passage is not attempting to function as a sex education class, we do not shrink from the questions that may be asked of us.

We believe that it is foolhardy to pretend to today's youth that sexuality does not exist. It accomplishes nothing and probably causes more damage to do so.

We also feel that it is important to discourage overt sexual activity among young people. In this way, not only can sexually transmitted diseases and unwanted pregnancies be avoided, but the psychic damage caused by indulging in behaviors more advanced than one's maturity can also be avoided.

The act of joining of Afrikan man and woman is a gift from the Creator. It (our sexuality) should not be taken lightly. It is sacred, as is the "fruit" of the union.

It has been shown repeatedly that homosexual activity is not natural to Afrika. It has been suggested that male and female homosexuality only occurs in rabid patriarchal societies. While we do not believe it to be in the best interests of Afrikan people to indulge in this deviant behavior, we do not reject those Afrikans who are addicted to those types of behaviors. In fact, there is some very preliminary suggestion that Rites of Passage can actually change some peoples' outlook on sexual orientation.

Black teenage pregnancy is another manifestation of alienation from our culture. As stated by our esteemed Elder, the late Dr. John Henrik Clarke, teenage pregnancy has always been a part of our culture. It had, however, rules that were followed to the letter, such as marriage first.

We have traditionally attacked this problem from a uniquely Eurocentric perspective. We blame the girls and concentrate most (if not all) of our efforts towards addressing their roles in the pregnancy as if they were the only players in the game.

The male role must be assigned major responsibility and must share in the consequences. However, Afrikan Centered Rites of Passage can markedly reduce the problem by instructing boys and girls before they make mistakes. They will be made aware of standardized expectations regarding conduct and will adhere to this as our Ancestors did and as our brothers and sisters in traditional Afrika do even today.

A good reference for the methods of one Afrikan ethnic group in approaching the sexuality is *Facing Mount Kenya: The Tribal Life of the Gikuyu* by Jomo Kenyatta.

Sexually Transmitted Diseases

At one point in the, not too distant, past, these illnesses were more a nuisance than a health threat. If one were to contract gonorrhea or syphilis (the major American STDs), all it took was a course of antibiotics, and you were as good as new. However, one of the problems with "progress" is that it brings other, less pleasant side effects. Gonorrhea developed some strains that were resistant to the usual antibiotics and even some that were totally resistant.

What also occurred was the emergence of viruses that could not be killed. Herpes simplex genitalis is extremely common in our community. Fortunately, it does not represent a danger to life but does cause a great deal of discomfort. It can be prevented by appropriate actions. The most appropriate action is avoidance of sexual intercourse completely until marriage. If one chooses to indulge in premarital sexual activity, however, knowledge of the cyclical nature of the infection MUST be known so that no sexual intercourse be experienced during periods of viral activity. Secondly, condoms are absolutely essential in order to prevent the spread of the Human Immunodeficiency Virus that has created a war zone in the area of Infectious Diseases. Again, the best way of dealing with this virus is sexual abstinence until marriage and then avoidance of extramarital intercourse. The group of people who are experiencing the greatest increase in infections is Afrikan women. Although significant advances in the treatment of HIV are being announced almost every day, there is no substitute for good common sense and caution. HIV infections are also being seen at earlier ages among all people but especially among Afrikan youth. Surveys repeatedly show that our youth ignore preventative measures and too frequently take risks that ultimately result in HIV infection.

Our youth must be made aware of their value to our collective future and must be made to see that casual sexual intercourse is not morally good or physically healthy. They must be given the strength to resist temptation so that the empty phrase, "Just say no," approaches reality.

Drug Use

This area of discussion can be divided into two main groups: legal drugs and illegal drugs. Also, if the concept of addiction is raised, addictions such as television, eating, and religion need to be discussed. However, our recommendation is that specific treatment of these topics is postponed until the second level of training.

The legal drugs that need to be discussed are tobacco (nicotine) and alcohol. We know that there are no real advantages to using tobacco in any form (smoking, chewing, or "dipping"). The addiction to tobacco is one of the most powerful physical addictions known to man, and there are people who have found it easier to stop using illegal drugs than to stop smoking cigarettes. Tobacco has been found to cause or contribute to cancer in areas such as the lung, esophagus, mouth, throat, and bladder. It contributes to several types of heart problems and also precipitates miscarriages. It causes emphysema and chronic bronchitis. Smoking causes a terrible odor in the clothes and hair of anyone close to the smoker as well as placing those people at risk for the development of the above-mentioned illnesses. Finally, smoking causes really bad breath. What reason is there to start smoking? If it does help calm the nerves, as many people claim, are calm nerves worth living with cancer, shortness of breath and having to keep oxygen on constantly?

Actually, alcohol could be placed in the category of illegal drugs for those people under the age of twenty-one. Alcohol is another drug that has few advantages. It also can contribute to empty lives. The physical consequences of alcohol abuse include severe liver disease (that triggers disease in other parts of the body) and contribute to cancers such as cancer of the esophagus.

Although there are far too many illegal drugs available in today's world, we frequently concentrate on two, marijuana and cocaine (although heroin is dealt with to some extent). Marijuana ("reefer" or "weed") is enjoying a "comeback" in popularity. Although there is no evidence that it is physically addicting, it does have many detrimental effects on motor activity as well as mental functioning. Those young people who use marijuana usually do poorly in school and have unfulfilling lives.

Cocaine is a double-edged trap for our young people. It has, unfortunately, attracted a mythology of glamour and money. We find many of our youth entangled in the destructive lifestyle of drug dealing. They understand the danger too late. In order to be successful, they have to completely buy into the materialistic ethics of today's world. They must be ready to kill or be killed and must have no respect for human life or suffering. This, for Afrikan people, is a profoundly severe manifestation of mental illness. The legal consequences are also devastating. The penalties for the use and sale of powder cocaine (used by more European-Americans) are much more lenient than those for use and sale of crack cocaine (used more by Afrikans in America). Hence, we have criminalization and mental illness/ mentacide in one fell swoop.

Cocaine addiction is one of the most intense addictions known to man. It destroys more lives than just the addicted individual. The family, friends, and community suffer from the loss of just one young life to addiction. Because of the seriousness of the addiction, the affected person will do anything in order to get drugs. This is not only very potentially violent, but also creates a situation in which these individuals can be exploited in every way known.

Frequent Illnesses in AUSA

There are several illnesses that are found in all people but have either an increased frequency or have a worse course in Afrikans. Diabetes Mellitus is one of these. It is one of the major causes (directly or indirectly) of blindness, heart disease, kidney failure requiring dialysis, strokes, and amputations in America. Although the predisposition to developing diabetes is genetic, there are several ways of potentially influencing the development and course of the disease. The first is to always observe good nutritional practices, eating sugar and fat in moderation as well as increasing dietary fiber intake. The second is to exercise regularly. If one has a family history of diabetes or has already been diagnosed as being diabetic, these measures, as well as faithfully taking medications prescribed by a physician, become even more important.

Our youth are confronted with family members daily with diabetes and frequently are in a position to help influence the health decision-making of their loved ones. Rites of Passage training helps them to assume this responsibility with a wider and more appropriate knowledge base.

Hypertension (high blood pressure) has been called "the silent killer" because it rarely causes symptoms until very late. It seems to be a different disease in Afrikans in America than in other people. There are many theories for this fact, but no one has been able to definitely prove any of them. What we are left with, however, is the fact that high blood pressure is a major factor in causing strokes, heart attacks, heart failure and kidney failure in our community. Again, the ways of optimally dealing with this disease are relatively simple. Eating correctly, exercising, and taking prescribed medicine regularly are of utmost importance. Patients are urged to monitor their own blood pressure and to communicate with their physicians regularly. Our youth are taught how to take blood pressure so that they may participate in the maintenance of the health of their families and communities.

More children are being born out of wedlock in the Afrikan community today than ever before. Unfortunately, young mothers are too often left with the entire responsibility of childcare. When others participate in the care of the baby, it is the grandparents who are called upon to provide the bulk of the care. The trainees in *Project: Sankofa!* are not only taught to face their responsibilities and accept the consequences of their actions but are taught the basics of caring for an infant. The boys and the girls are given the same information so that they can be responsible for the life that they have created. Even if they are not parents, the practical application of this information can help prepare them to earn money as babysitters.

One recurring theme in this entire chapter has been the focus on the importance of good nutrition. While we do not advocate any particular food lifestyle (e.g., vegetarianism or avoiding pork), we respect those ideas and their proponents. In reality, the basic optimal nutrition does support many of the dietary practices found among diet-conscious Afrikan people.

We feel that the optimal diet is one that is low fat, high fiber with minimal concentrated carbohydrates (sugar) and salt. This diet does actually reduce the amount of meat (of any type) that is ingested while increasing the amount of vegetables ingested. This diet also practically eliminates "fast food" in the diet. Unfortunately, these "fast foods" have become staples in the diets of almost all Americans but are exceedingly unhealthy. If we can convince our youth to eat more responsibly, not only will our communities become healthier, but we will also send an economic message to the fast food chains that they should improve their products.

Exercise is also an invaluable and almost a miracle activity. Exercise not only helps the heart and lungs; it also is associated with lower incidence of various cancers.

When the trainees learn this information, as well as other hygienic information, they will become health monitors and teaches at home. The community is then helped.

Science and Technology

This section would not be complete without a cursory mention of the contribution that Afrika and Afrikans have had to science and technology. Any consideration of Africans and Science, Invention, and Technology must be viewed within the cultural container in which it flourished. Without consideration of history and culture, it becomes very difficult to imagine that formerly enslaved Afrikans could have contributed so much to the scientific and technological advancement of this country. It is even more difficult to realize how much was done just after the civil war.

Science, as it is defined in the western world, is the inquiry into nature and the study of why and how the world works as it does. As previously stated, Afrikans saw themselves in harmonious relationships with nature. Afrikans had a curiosity about nature, and they wondered how and why things worked just as Europeans and Asians did. However, the motivation of Afrikans was to develop a clearer understanding of the God-force. They felt that in a harmonious relationship with nature, God would reveal herself to them. It is through this cultural window that one must see the totality of Afrikans in science, invention and technology.

It has only been two decades since archeologists discovered the lost African sciences in areas outside of ancient Kemet (Egypt). As early as 4246 B.C.E., these Afrikans had developed an accurate calendar, the basis of which we still use. Three hundred years before the birth of

Christ, Kenyans had a complex astronomical observatory. The chief result of this was a highly sophisticated and complex but accurate calendar system. In order to achieve these innovations, excellence in complex mathematics and astronomy had to be common. The development of a calendar also means that sophisticated record-keeping over long periods of time was achieved.

The ancient Afrikans also excelled in shipbuilding, which requires mathematics, physics and engineering. The ancient Chinese have recorded that Afrikans visited China in ships. As early as the thirteen century, Africans were shipping elephants to China, two hundred years before the Columbus expedition to the so-called "new world."

Afrikan science has had a great impact on agriculture. Africans were cultivating cotton as early as 3500 B.C. This would also indicate that Africans had been to America long before Columbus took his journey.

There is some evidence suggesting that Afrikans had domesticated cattle some 15,000 years ago. Grain was used 8000 years ago domestically. If the domestication of cattle is a key indicator of civilization, then this is more proof of Afrika's primary position in the history of the world.

In the field of metallurgy, Afrikans have shown tremendous advancement. Afrikans living on the western shores of Lake Nyanza (Victoria) in Tanzania 1500-2000 years ago produced carbon steel. The furnaces used for producing this carbon steel were technologically more advanced and complex than anything developed in Europe until the mid-19th century.

This technology was not limited to Tanzania. There sems to have been many iron smelting industrial sites throughout the region. In order for this type of industry to have flourished, the people who developed this technology had to live in densely populated areas with an organized labor force. This would indicate that the formation of cities with complex social systems was already in place in order to accommodate this industry and its organized labor force.

It is well documented that the practice of medicine existed in an advanced empirical and theoretical state as early as 5000 years ago in Afrika. The scientific achievements of Afrika: astronomy, physics, mathematics, engineering, medicine, nautical and navigational science, agriculture, and metallurgy show that creative scientific and technological genius has always been a part of our history. It is through this prism that we understand the continuity of science, invention, and technology by Afrikans here in America.

When one takes into account the dehumanizing hardships that Afrikans endured during and after the period of enslavement in America, one becomes awed when the contributions of Afrikans in the field of science and invention here in America are considered. In 1870 more than 80% of the African community could not read or write their own name. One-third of the Afrikan population here in America some 40 years later who were over the age of 10 still had not ever been to school. It is against this backdrop of educational deprivation that the contribution to the advancement of life here in America should be seen.

This lack of formal education was not the only obstacle Afrikan scientists and inventors encountered. There were innumerable legal and social problems as well. In pre-civil war America, enslaved Afrikans were unable to obtain patents. There is no way today to determine the actual number of Afrikan inventors who had their inventions stolen by their slave masters. Free Afrikans were also frequently denied patents once their racial identities were known.

Even though many of the inventions by Afrikans here in America may never be known, the ones we can verify would number in the thousands.

The health of Ausa people and, indeed, Afrikan people all over the world is deteriorating despite technical advances in medical science. Much of this is related to a lack of information. Young people need to be made aware of the health results of their actions. It is also important to relate the history of medical science to its Afrikan beginnings. In this way, more brilliant Afrikan minds may be drawn to careers in health that can have positive implications for all people of Afrikan heritage.

Potential Behavioral Problems

Often young people are referred to Rites of Passage Programs because they have behavioral problems and deemed "at-risk". We should always remember that these problems do not occur in a vacuum. There is almost always something that stimulates these behavioral problems. The formal name for these experiences is Adverse Childhood Experiences or ACE, but we just call them trauma. To be black in America is to be exposed to psychological trauma constantly. There are three types of these experiences:

1. Abuse, which can be physical, emotional, or sexual;
2. Neglect, which can be physical or emotional;
3. Household dysfunction can be mental illness, an incarcerated relative, divorce, substance abuse, or being treated violently by a parent.

The signs of these traumas manifest in different ways, from aggressively acting out and open defiance to complete withdrawal and refusing to engage or participate.

> The relatively new science of Epigenetics has shown that the effects of trauma can be passed down through generations. So, many of these young people are experiencing personal trauma that is "piled" on top of trauma passed to them from their ancestors. This is

what Dr. Joy DeGruy calls "Post Traumatic Slave Syndrome".

When presented with these behavioral problems, we have found two things to be of help:

1. The young people should understand that you love them. Because ROP Programs rarely pay well, it should be understood that your efforts are a labor of love, love for them.
2. It is absolutely essential that these young people trust you. They should know that you have their best interests at heart.

It is equally important that the trainer realizes that when the problems with the young people go beyond their expertise, it is imperative to consult trained professionals.

Materials: Same as previous Units

Didactic: Discussion of Sexually Transmitted Diseases
Discussion of the effects of drugs:

- marijuana (weed, hash, pot, ganja, grass)
- crack cocaine
- alcohol
- cocaine
- tobacco use
- Fentanyl
- Ecstasy (MDMA, E, crystal)
- Ketamine
- LSD (acid, blotter)

- Magic mushrooms (shrooms, mushies)
- methamphetamine (meth, crank, ice)
- heroin (smack, skag)

Common illnesses of Ausa

- Diabetes mellitus (sugar)
- Hypertension and strokes
- Infections
- Cancer
- Asthma
- Strokes

Parenting and childcare
Dietary choices/Nutrition

Experiential: Teaching how to take blood pressure. Using dolls, care of babies will be taught.

Media: The Immortal Life of Henrietta-Lacks
Miss Evers boys

Biography: Charles Drew
Daniel Hale Williams
Imhotep

Literature: Flyers will be given to the trainees with regard to the topics chosen.

Field Trip: The trainees will be taken to a hospital and/or clinic for a tour. They will also be exposed to

	other health delivery systems and laboratories.
Expected Outcome:	Upon completion of this Unit, the trainees will become more aware of the relationship between their actions and their health. They will develop more respect for their bodies as well as their minds. They will not only be drug-free but will use their knowledge and influence to induce their peers to become drug-free and healthy.

Didactic

Many, if not most, of the health problems suffered by people of Afrikan origin in America are the result of specific behaviors. Many, if not most, of these illnesses and conditions could be prevented or, at least, improved with dietary change, cessation of harmful activities, and moderation in other activities.

It is important to impress upon the trainees the importance of good nutrition. It is equally important to teach them the difference between nutritional avoidance of some food and cultural/religious avoidance of some food so that they may make informed decisions.

The genetic basis for some illnesses (some cancers, diabetes mellitus, heart disease, and sickle cell anemia) should be discussed.

The relationship of smoking to cancer, heart disease, and birth defects is important to know as well as the obvious pitfalls of drugs and alcohol.

With regard to sexually transmitted diseases (STDs), abstinence is the best answer, by far. However, realistically, some of our youth have already begun sexual activity or will start experimenting. Therefore, it is imperative that they be taught methods of prevention of STDs (as well as contraception).

Drug usage is a major problem in both urban and rural areas. It is important that our youth be alerted to the dangers of all drugs (including alcohol and tobacco). The relationship between tobacco and health is spotlighted (association with various types of cancer, heart disease, fetal distress, and lung diseases, especially).

Nutritional issues are not spotlighted enough. The relationship of specific nutritional habits with disease will be spotlighted (such as the relationship between eating high fat, low fiber foods with colon cancer and the association of diets high in cholesterol with heart attacks). The trainees should be made aware of the experimentation on black bodies during and after slavery as well as the scientific racism this supported this abuse.

Experiential

To illustrate how simple and important some health procedures can be, the trainees will learn how to use a sphygmomanometer and measure blood pressure.

Patients with AIDS, cancer, and other illnesses will be brought to speak with the trainees. Medical specialists will give talks and demonstrations and be available to answer questions about health and specific issues.

Giving Our Children Back to the Community: The Graduation Ceremony

At the conclusion of a Rites of Passage program, a graduation is conducted. There is usually Afrikan drumming, ritual, speeches, awards, and presentations of gifts to the trainees. This is done in the presence of parents and community people. Following the public ceremony, there usually is a short reception, banquet, or planned meal.

But it is what leads up to the graduation, which is really important. Each child has gone through forty to ninety hours of training, learning, thinking, and growing. Each child has been exposed to more understanding of their culture and history than most Afrikan people will learn in a lifetime. Each child has the rudiments of a new identity and, at least, an understanding that a purposeful life is planned and disciplined.

Through this exposure and challenge to their intellect and emotions, each trainee has grown or stepped upon the path of growth. Most will never be satisfied with the lack of information which will come to them from various sources. Some will challenge these sources and will cause the sources to either grow or become angry. If the trainee has learned well, they will be able to handle both reactions appropriately.

At home, now, the new graduate possesses knowledge that many of their parents do not. They have been taught that this information is for the benefit and positive growth of their families and communities. They have pledged continually to assist and respect family. These graduates, through the knowledge obtained, will increase family wealth and stability if they use the information wisely.

Prior to the public ceremony, the private wisdom of the trainee is tested. Though each of them has functioned almost completely as a group throughout the Rites of Passage program, the moment of truth is when their knowledge is tested individually. Each trainee is led, individually, before the elders, who question his or her knowledge by using a riddle. The trainee is tested to ascertain the ability to think, reason, and to make logical and correct choices, independent of a supportive group of their age-grade peers.

Many trainees feel that this event is the most difficult of all lessons and experiences during the Rites of Passage training. They had learned that working together was comfortable and made tasks easier to accomplish. This is provided that the goal of the task is clearly stated, and that goal is for the positive benefit of the group. However, what happens when an individual is confronted with a problem, and there is no support group there to assist? The calm and poise taught to the trainees should assist them. If the training has been valid and reached them, then the answer to the problem is simple.

Most solve the riddle without prompting and go on to do well in other things. The rest have solved the riddle after some coaxing. As a trainer, you never know who will answer the riddle. However, these usually are the best graduates and will go on to lead others positively.

The reaction of parents to their children, who have gone through the Rites of Passage training, is important and instructive. Many children have been placed in Rites of Passage programs because their parents feel that they are bad, need saving, or they feel that the program can provide something they cannot. To a certain degree, the parents have done right by placing a child in a Rites of Passage program because the practice itself is culture-based. However, and probably more importantly, Rites of Passage programs, if formulated correctly, are about raising adults by assisting the child through the transition from childhood to adulthood.

Stated another way, parents raise children, while Rites of Passage programs raise adults. Parents send a child, and more times than now, a new person emerges at graduation.

Parents on many occasions have come to the authors and stated that we had given their children back to them. What was given back was not a child but a budding adult who had ventured onto the right path.

The right path for an adult is to adhere to pledges. You see, nothing just happens, and the pledge is the key. All those good things we want out of our children, we get by design, planning, and diligence. When the details get murky, we fall back to the pledge as a guide. For what is an adult but a person who is able and willing to carry out all that is promised.

The Day of Passage

The Day of Passage is the longest day of the Rites of Passage Program. There are four main parts to the day, firstly, the Ritual of Preparedness; secondly, the preparation; thirdly, The Passage Ceremony; and lastly, the Karamu (feast).

The Ritual of Preparedness

During this ritual, each trainee is solemnly brought into a separate room, alone, with one or more of the trainers. Several items are placed on a desk or a table. Each item should have cultural value peculiar to Afrikan or Afrikan American culture. In a very formal and ritualized manner, the trainee will be asked a series of questions about the items. The answers should be fairly simple and straightforward and should relate to the values and principles that they have been taught. The answers should also relate to protecting the community and respecting elders and members of the opposite sex. This exercise should take from 15-30 minutes (depending on the size of the group).

Upon successful completion of this ritual, the trainee is taken back with the group and is cautioned not to discuss what happened or what was said.

The Preparation

After everyone has completed the Ritual of Preparation, each trainee is given an assignment to practice for the actual passage ceremony. This should include reciting the Principles of Maat, the Virtues, and the Nguzo Saba. Recitation and interpretation of one or more of the poems studied could also be done but should be practiced thoroughly during the time between the Ritual of Preparation and the Ceremony of passage.

The Ceremony of Passage

This ceremony should be public and very ritualized and all the relatives, friends, and other concerned associates of the trainees specifically invited.

The ceremony should be designed so that all the trainers and trainees participate. A prayer and libation should start the ceremony. A brief description of the length of the program should be given.

The ceremony should not be too long and should not take more than 30-45 minutes. The parents (especially the mother or a surrogate mother) should participate in the ceremony. Sometimes a guest speaker might add greatly to the Ceremony.

A certificate should be presented to each trainee completing the program. They should also be given other items that specifically signify their completion of the project. A specially designed t-shirt is optimal. A strip of kente cloth is also a significant award.

Afrikan drumming at various points during the ceremony adds tremendously to the aura and solemnity and is strongly recommended.

The Karamu (feast)

Following the Ceremony of Passage, the trainers, trainees, families, and other members of the audience should be invited to a Karamu. This is a sort of debriefing and gives the families and trainers the opportunity to observe the former trainees in their new personages. It is usually a happy and light-hearted occasion that is a fitting end to the serious material that has been made a major part of the former trainees' lives.

Follow-up

The trainers should actively maintain close contact with the graduates, preferably indefinitely and be willing to provide as much support as they need.

Program Evaluation

1. Pre and Post tests.
2. Parental evaluation.
3. Audits (qualitative from quantitative).
4. Use a reference group.

Bibliography and Suggested Reading for Project Sankofa

The * indicates those references that can be read and used by the youth early in the process.

The ** indicates those references that must be read by trainers (NOTE: Trainers must also read and be familiar with the books recommended for the youth).

The # indicates those references that have a curriculum that can be used or an extended bibliography.

Aaronson, Bernard. "Timeless Minds". *Omni*, February 1984

**Abdullah Samella. *Posttraumatic Stress Disorder: A Diagnosis for Victims of the African Holocaust: United States of America Component*, Chicago: African World Community Press, 1994

Addae, Erriel Kofi (editor). *To Heal A People: Afrikan Scholars Defining a New Reality*, Columbia, MD Kujichagulia Press, 1996

*Adams, Russell L. *Great Negroes: Past and Present*, Chicago: Afro-Am Publishing Co., 1984

*Akbar, Na'im. Mental Disorder Among African Americans, *Black Books Bulletin* 7:2, 1981

**Akbar, Na'im. *Chains and Images of Psychological Slavery*, Jersey City: New Mind Publications, 1984

*Akbar, Na'im. *Light from Ancient Africa*, Tallahassee: Mind Productions and Associates, Inc., 1994

*Akbar, Na'im. *Visions for Black Men,* Nashville: Winston-Derek Publishers, Inc., 1991

**Akbar, Na'im. Mental Disorder Among African Americans in *Black Psychology,* Editor: Berkeley: Reginald Jones, Cobbs and Henry Publishers, 1991

**Akoto, Kwame Agyei. *Nationbuilding: Theory and Practice in Afrikan Centered Education,* Washington: Pan Afrikan World Institute, 1992

#Ani, Marimba. Yurugu: *An African-Centered Critique of European Cultural Thought and Behavior,* Trenton: Africa World Press, 1994

Ani, Marimba. *Let the Circle be Unbroken,* NY: Nkonimfo Publications, 1997

**Armah, Ayi Kwei. *Two Thousand Seasons,* New Hampshire: Heinemann Educational Books, Inc., 1973

*Armah, Ayi Kwei. *The Healers,* New Hampshire: Heinemann Educational Books, Inc., 1979

Asante, Molefi K. and Kariamu W. Asante (editors). *African Culture: The Rhythms of Unity,* London: Greenwood Press, 1985

**Asante, Molefi Kete. *Afrocentricity,* Trenton: Africa World Press, Inc., 1988

**Asante, Molefi Kete. Kemet, Afrocentricity and Knowledge, Trenton: Africa World Press, 1990

Azibo, Daudi Ajani Ya. African-Centered Theses on Mental Health and a Nosology of Black/African personality Disorder. *Journal of Black Psychology* 15: 173-214, 1989

*Barashango, Rev. Ishakamusa. *African People and European Holidays: A Mental Genocide,* Washington: IV Dynasty Publishing Co., 1980

*Bell, Derrick. *Faces at the Bottom of the Well: The Permanence of Racism,* NY: BasicBooks, 1992

Bell, Yvonne R. A Culturally Sensitive Analysis of Black Learning Style, *Journal of Black Psychology* 20 (1): 47-61, 1994

Bennett, Jr., Lerone. *Before the Mayflower: A History of Black America,* NY: Penguin Books, 1985

Brookins, Craig C. and Tracy L. Robinson. Rites of Passage as Resistance to Oppression, *The Western Journal of Black Studies,* Volume 19, 1995

#*Browder, Anthony T. *From the Browder File: 22 Essays on the African American Experience,* Washington: The Institute of Karmic Guidance, 1989

**Browder, Anthony T. *Exploding the Myths, Volume 1: Nile Valley Contributions to Civilization,* Washington: The Institute of Karmic Guidance, 1992

* Browder, Anthony T. (*From the Browder File, Volume II: Survival Strategies for Afrikans in America: 13 Steps to Freedom,* Washington: The Institute of Karmic Guidance, 1996

*Browder, Atlantis, Tiye. *My First Trip to Africa,* Washington: The Institute of Karmic Guidance, 1991

Burt, Della. The Legacy of the Bad Nigger, *Journal of Afro-American Issues*, Vol. 5, Number 2, Spring, 1977

Burt, McKinley, Jr. (1969): *Black Inventors of America.* Portland: National Book Company, 1969

Carruthers, Jacob H. Essays in Ancient Egyptian Studies, Los Angeles: University of Sankore Press, 1984

Carruthers, Jacob H. and Leon Harris. *African World History Project: The Preliminary Challenge,* Los Angeles: Association for the Study of Classical African Civilizations, 1997

*Clarke, John Henrik: *African People in World History,* Baltimore: Black Classic Press,

Clarke, John Henrik. *Notes for An African World Revolution: Africans at the Crossroads,* Trenton: Africa World Press, 1991

#Clarke, John Henrik and Yosef ben-Jochannon. *New Dimensions in African History,* Trenton: Africa World Press, Inc., 1991

Cohen, Jeff and Norman Solomon. *Through the Media Looking Glass: Decoding Bias and Blather in the News,* Monroe, ME: Common Courage Press, 1995

Connor, Marlene Kim. *What is Cool?: Understanding Black Manhood in America,* NY: Crown Publishers, Inc., 1995

The Council of Independent Black Institutions Social Studies Curriculum. *Positive Afrikan Images for Children,* Trenton: The Red Sea Press, 1990

Dates, Jannette L. and William Barlow (editors) (1993): *Split Image: African Americans in the Mass Media,* Howard University Press, Washington, D.C.

DeGruy, Joy. *Post Traumatic Slave Syndrome: America's Legacy of Enduring Injury & Healing*. Stone Mountain: Joy DeGruy Publications, Inc., 2017

Dick, Robert C. *Black Protest: Issues and Tactics,* Westport: Westport: Greenwood Press, 1974

Diop, Cheikh Anta. *African Origins of Civilization: Myth or Reality,* Lawrence Hill and Company, 1974

Diop, Cheikh Anta. *The Cultural Unity of Black Africa,* Chicago: Third World Press, 1978

Diop, Cheikh Anta. *Civilization or Barbarism: An Authentic Anthropology,* NY: Lawrence Hill Books, 1991, pp. 283-284

Fanon, Frantz. *The Wretched of the Earth.* NY: Grove Press, 2005

Fanon, Frantz. *Black Skins, White Masks.* NY: Grove Press, 2008

Finch, Charles S. Imhotep, the Physician: Archetype of the Great Man, In: Great Black Leaders: Ancient and Modern (editor: Ivan Van Sertima), *Journal of African Civilizations,* Volume 9, pp. 213-231, 1987

Finch, Charles, S. *The African Background to Medical Science: Essays on African History, Science, and Civilization,* London: Karmak House,1990

** Finch, Charles S. *Echoes of the Old Darkland: Themes from the African Eden*, Decatur, GA: Khenti, Inc., 1991

Finch, Charles S. III, MD. *The Star of Deep Beginnings: The Genesis of African Science and technology*, Decatur, GA: Khenti, Inc., 1998

** Fu-Kiau, Kimbuandende Kia Bunseki. *Self-Healing Power and Therapy: Old Teachings from Africa*, NY: Vantage Press, 1991

Gallman, Burnett W. *Innervisions: Rx for Survival for People of Afrikan Origin*, Columbia: Imhotep Enterprises, 1994

Gallman, Burnett Kwadwo: *Sankofa University: Studying African Centered History and Culture.* Columbia: Imhotep-The Drum, 2020

Gunn, Jr., William. African Spirituality and Rhythmic Movement, In: *Voices from AARI-SC: Offerings on Afrikan Life* (Editor: Burnett W. Gallman, Jr.), Columbia: Imhotep Enterprises, 1993

* Haber, Louis. *Black Pioneers of Science and Invention*, NY: Harcourt Brace and Company, San Diego, 1970

Harris, Shanette M. Black Male Masculinity and Same-sex Friendships, *Western Journal of Black Studies* 16(2): 74-81, 1992

Henry, Charles P. The Political Role of the "Bad Nigger," *Journal of Black Studies*, Vol. 11, pp. 461-482, 1981

**Hill, Paul Jr. *Coming of Age: African American Male Rites of Passage*, Chicago: African American Images, 1992

** Hill, Paul Jr. Back to the Future, *Journal of African American Men*, 1(1): 41-62, 1995

**Hilliard, Asa G. III. Kemetic Concepts in Education. (From: Nile Valley Civilizations, Ed.: Ivan Van Sertima), *Journal of African Civilizations*, Volume 6, Number 2, 1984

** Hilliard, Asa G. III. *Pedagogy in Ancient Kemet*. (*In Kemet and the African Worldview: Research, Rescue, and Restoration*, Editors: Maulana Karenga and Jacob Carruthers), Los Angeles: University of Sankore Press, 1986

* Hilliard, Asa G. III, Larry Williams, and Nia Damali (editors). *The Teachings of Ptahhotep: The Oldest Book in the World*, Atlanta: Blackwood Press and Company, Inc. 1987

Hilliard, Asa G. III, Lucretia Payton-Stewart, Larry Obadele Williams (1990): *Infusion of African and African American Content in the School Curriculum: Proceedings of the First National Conference*, October 1989, Morristown, NJ: Aaron Press,

** Hilliard, Asa G. *The Maroon Within Us: Selected Essays on African American Community Socialization*, Baltimore: Black Classic Press, 1995

Hilliard, Asa G. III: *Fifty References on the History of Afrikan People*, Baltimore: Black Classic Press, 1993

** Hilliard, Asa G. *SBA: The Reawakening of the African Mind*, Gainesville, FL: Makare Publishing Company, 1997

Houston, Druscilla Dungee. *Those Wonderful Ethiopians of the Kushite Empire*. Baltimore: Black Classic Press, 1985

Hunter, Andrea G. and James Earl Davis. Hidden Voices of Black Men: The Meaning, Structure, and Complexity of Manhood, *Journal of Black Studies*, Vol. 25, pp. 20-40, 1994

Hutchinson, Earl Ofari. *Black Fatherhood: The Guide to Male Parenting*, Los Angeles: Middle Passage Press, 1994

Hutchinson, Earl Ofari. *Black Fatherhood II, Black Women Talk About Their Men*, Los Angeles: Middle Passage Press, 1995

**Hutchinson, Earl Ofari. *The Assassination of the Black Male Image*, Los Angeles: Middle Passage Press, 1994

Jackson, John G. *Introduction to African Civilizations*, Secaucus: The Citadel Press, 1970

Jackson, Ronald L. II. Black "Manhood" as Xenophobe: An Ontological Exploration of the Hegelian Dialectic, *Journal of Black Studies* 27(6):731-750, 1997

James, George G.M. *Stolen Legacy*, San Francisco: Julian Richardson Associates,

Kafele, Baruti K. *A Black Parent's Handbook to Educating Your Children (Outside of the Classroom)*, Fords, NJ: Baruti Publishing, 1991

**Kambon, Kobi Kazembe Kalongi. *The African Personality in America: An African-Centered Framework*, Tallahassee: Nubian Nation Publications, 1992

**Kenyatta, Jomo. *Facing Mount Kenya: The Tribal Life of the Gikuyu*, NY: Vintage Press, 1978 (First published in 1938)

Karenga, Maulana. *Introduction to Black Studies*, Los Angeles. University of Sankore Press, 1982

* Karenga, Maulana. *Selections from the Husia: Sacred Wisdom of Ancient Egypt*, Los Angeles: University of Sankore Press, 1984

Lee, Courtland. Successful African American Male Youth: A Psychological Profile, *Journal of African American Men*, 1(3): 63-72, 1995

**Madhubuti, Haki R. *Black Men: Obsolete, Single, Dangerous?: The African American Family in Transition: Essays in Discovery, Solution and Hope*, Chicago: Third World Press, 1990

Majors, Richard and Janet Mancini Billson. *Cool Pose: The Dilemmas of Black Manhood in America*. NY: A Touchstone Book, Published by Simon & Schuster, 1992

McAdoo, Harriette Pipes (editor). *Black Families*, Newberry Park: Sage Publications, 1988

* Middleton, Listervelt. *Southern Winds, African Breezes*, Columbia: Seamon Publications, 1987

* Morrison, Toni. *The Bluest Eye*. NY: Plume/Penguin Books, 1994

Mutisya P. Masila. Demythologization and Demystification of African Initiation Rites: A Positive and Meaningful Educational Aspect Heading for Extinction, *Journal of Black Studies* 27(1): 94-103, 1996

**Myers, Linda James. The Deep Structure of Culture: Relevance of Traditional African Culture in Contemporary Life, *Journal of Black Studies* 18(1): 72-85, 1987

Nantambu, Kwame (aka Linus A. Hoskins). *Decoding European Geopolitics: Afrocentric Perspectives,* Kent, Ohio: Imhotep Publishing Company, 1994

Nichols, Elaine: *A Spark of Genius, Medicine, Science and Creative Thought in South Carolina,* Columbia: South Carolina State Museum,

Nobles, Wade W. (1985): *Africanity and the Black Family: The Development of a Theoretical Model,* A Black Family Institute Publication, P.O. Box 24739, CA 94623

**Nobles, Wade W. *African Psychology: Toward Its Reclamation, Reascension and Revitalization,* Oakland: A Black Family Institute Publication, 1986

** Oliver, William. Black Males and Social Problems: Prevention Through Afrocentric Socialization, *Journal of Black Studies,* Vol. 20, pp. 15-39, 1998

Opoku, Kofi Asare. *West African Traditional Religion,* Accra: Fep International Private, Limited, 1978

Pearson, Dale F. The Black Man: health Issues and Implications for Clinical Practice, *Journal of Black Studies,* Vol. 25, No. 1, pp. 81-98, 1994

* Perkins, Useni Eugene. *Afrocentric Self Inventory and Discovery Workbook for African American Youth,* Chicago: Third World Press,1989

* Person-Lynn, Kwaku. *First Word: Black Scholars, Thinkers, Warriors: Knowledge, Wisdom, Mental Liberation,* Chicago: Harlem River Press, 1996

* Randall, Dudley (editor): *The Black Poets,* NY: Bantom Books, 1971

Roberts, George W. Brother to Brother: African American Modes of Relating Among Men, *Journal of Black Studies,* Vol. 24, 1994, pp. 379-390, 1994

* Rodney, Walter. *How Europe Underdeveloped Africa,* Washington: Howard University Press, 1982

* Rogers, J.A. *Africa's Gift to America,* St. Petersburg, FL: Helga M. Rogers, 1961

* Rogers, J.A. *World's Great Men of Color,* (two volumes) NY: Collier Books, 1972

* Rogers, J.A. *World's Great Men of Color,* (two volumes) NY: Collier Books, 1972

Some', Malidoma Patrice. *Ritual: Power, Healing and Community,* Portland: Swan/(Raven & Company), 1993

Staples, Robert. *Black Masculinity: The Black Man's Role in American Society,* San Francisco: The Black Scholar Press, 1988

Stuckey, Sterling. *Slave Culture: Nationalist Theory and the Foundations of Black America,* NY: Oxford University Press, 1987

Turner, Patricia A. *Ceramic Uncles and Celluloid Mammies: Black Images and Their Influence on Culture,* NY: Anchor Books, 1994

* Van Sertima, Ivan (editor): *Journal of African Civilizations*, Transaction Publishers, New Brunswick, NJ, The following issues:

African Presence in Early Asia
African Presence in Early Europe
Blacks in Science: Ancient and Modern
Black Women in Antiquity
Egypt Revisited
Golden Age of the Moor
Great Black Leaders: Ancient and Modern
African Presence in Early America
Great African Thinkers: Cheikh Anta Diop
Egypt: Child of Africa

** Warfield-Coppock, Nsenga and Aminifu R. Harvey. *A Rites of Passage Resource Manual*, Washington: Maat Institute for Human and Organizational Enhancement, Inc., 1989

Watkins-Beatty, Valethia

Welsing, Frances Cress. *The Isis papers: The Keys to the Colors.* Bensenville, IL: Lushena Books, 2004

Warren, Lee. The Dance of Africa, NY: Prentice-Hall, 1972

* Williams, Chancellor. *The Destruction of Black Civilization: Great Issues of a Race from 4500 B.C. to 2000* A.D. Chicago: Third World Press, 1976

** Williams, Larry Obadele (Unpublished Manuscript): *Africana Manhood Training: A Rites of Passage Structure, Process and Practice*

Williams, Reginald. Biblio-Mentors: Autobiography as a Tool for Counseling African American Males, *Journal of African American Men*, 1(3): 73-83, 1995/96

Williams, Robert L. *An Afro-Centric Theory of Black Personality*, St. Louis: Williams and Associates, Inc., 1981

Wilson, Amos N. *Black-on-Black Violence: The Psychodynamics of Black Self-Annihilation in Service of White Domination*, NY: Afrikan World InfoSystems, 1990

**Wilson, Amos N. *Understanding Black Adolescent Male Violence: Its Remediation and Prevention*, NY: Afrikan World InfoSystems, 1992

** Wilson, Amos N. *Awakening the Natural Genius of Black Children*, NY: Afrikan World InfoSystems, 1992

** Wilson, Amos N. *The Falsification of Afrikan Consciousness: Eurocentric History, Psychiatry and the Politics of White Supremacy*, NY: Afrikan World InfoSystems, 1993

** Woodson, Carter G. *The Mis-Education of the Negro*, Washington: The Associated Publishers, 1933

**Wright, Bobby: *Mentacide: The Ultimate Threat to the Black Race*, (Unpublished Manuscript)

Glossary: Words to Guide You Home: A Journey of Self Discovery

ABPsy	The Association of Black Psychologists, an Afrikan Centered organization dedicated to healing Afrikan People from the psychic injuries suffered during the Maafa.
Adinkra	A series of symbols originating in the Asante (Ashanti) region of Ghana that often have profound meanings.
Aesthetics	Simply put, this refers to the theory of what a person or group finds attractive or beautiful, or to their taste. It is regarded by many as the newest branch of the philosophical tree of humanity.
Afrik	Baba Hannibal Afrik is an esteemed Elder who has dedicated his life to the advancement of Afrikan people in America. Born in Greenville, SC, he lived most of his life in Chicago, where he was instrumental in the workings of The Republic of New Afrika.
Afrika	The second largest continent on the planet. It is the place of origin for those pigmented people on Earth called Afrikan, no matter where

they may be found. The word is spelled here using a "k" instead of a "c" in keeping with the linguistic rules of most Afrikan languages.

Afrikan Centered — Seeing the world from the perspective of an Afrikan person before colonization, enslavement, and oppression. Western education trains us to see the world from a Western (European) perspective. We really need to be able to see the world from our own perspective and for our own good. *Also called "Afrocentric".*

Age Grade — Groupings of students that include a 2-4 year difference in age. These groups team together and are taught to respect older age grades and teach younger age grades. *They maintain relationships throughout their lives.*

Agoo — An Asante Twi word that is spoken from the outside as a request to enter a room or building. It is pronounced "Ah-Goh". Among Ausa, it is used in order to call a gathering or meeting to order, get attention in a busy situation or to request silence. The response is "Amee" (pronounced "Ah-May".

Akan A group of peoples found mostly in Ghana, West Afrika that are related. The ethnic groups that make up the Akan people are the Asante (frequently called Ashanti), Fante (frequently called Fanti), Akuapim, Akyim (pronounced and frequently spelled "Akim", Kwahu, Brong, Denkyira (pronounced Den-cheer-rah), Nkonya, Ahafo, Wassaw, Nzema and Ntchumuru.

Akbar Na'im Akbar, Ph.D. is a premier theoretical and experimental Afrikan Centered psychologist, lecturer and author. He is based at the Florida State University in Tallahassee, FL.

Akua Chike Akua is a Master Teacher and educational consultant based in Atlanta, Georgia.

Allen *Richard Allen,* born, a slave, in 1760 in Philadelphia, PA, his mother and three siblings were sold away when he was 17 years old, and he never saw them again. He worked extra hours on the farm and bought his own freedom at age 20. He helped organize the Free African Society along with Absalom Jones in order to improve the social and economic condition of Black people in Philadelphia. He saved many lives during the Yellow Fever Epidemic of 1793 in Philadelphia. He organized the first institution just for Afrikan people in America in 1794: The African Methodist Episcopal (A.M.E.) Church and was its first bishop. He helped to organize the Negro Convention Movement by having the first meeting at Bethel Church in Philadelphia. He died in 1831.

Amee See Agoo

Ancestors Refers to those who have died and/or who have not yet been born. They are the intermediaries between the Creator and humans. They must be respected, *revered,* and *venerated.*

Ani Marimba Ani, Ph.D. (aka Dona Richards) is an Anthropologist, Educator, and Activist whose two primary books are of prime importance in Ausa understanding of themselves and European culture.

Ankh An ancient Afrikan (Kemetic) symbol that means "life." It celebrated the sanctity of life created together by woman and man. It is not an Afrikan cross or a satanic symbol.

Areas of Human Activity — According to Dr. Frances Cress Welsing, these are areas in which all human groups must participate. They are Economics, Education, Entertainment, Labor, Law, Politics, Religion, Sex, and War.

Armah — Ayi Kwei Armah is a prolific Ghanaian novelist and intellectual who has written many profound historical novels analyzing the history and values of ancient Afrikans as opposed to medieval Afrikans.

Art — Created things of form and/or beauty, including painting, sculpture, architecture, music, literature, drama, dance, entertainment, and sports.

Asa — The act of doing something that is correct, performing highest quality scholarship, down-to-earth intellectual leadership and "Good Speech" (liberating oratory). It refers to the profoundly brilliant contributions of Asa G. Hilliard, III, who was one of the brightest lights and most effective intellectual warriors of Afrikan Centered scholarship. The designation was suggested by Dr. Wade W. Nobles, another one of intellectual warrior-leaders.

Asante	An Afrikan ethnic group. Frequently called Ashanti, and found mostly in the mountains of central Ghana, West Afrika. They were a warlike member of the Akan people.
Asante	Molefi Kete Asante is the former chair of Afrikana Studies, Temple University in Philadelphia, PA, the first American university to offer a Ph.D. in Black studies. He has authored many books and articles and is one of the first to define and use the term "Afrocentricity."
Asante Day Names	Many Akan people give their children names that symbolize the day of the week on which they were born. These names are:

Day	*Male Name*	*Female Name*
Monday	*Kwadwo*	*Adwoa*
Tuesday	*Kwabena*	*Abenaa*
Wednesday	*Kwaku*	*Akua*
Thursday	*Yaw*	*Yaa*
Friday	*Kofi*	*Afua*
Saturday	*Kwame*	*Amma*
Sunday	*Kwasi*	*Akosua*

Asantewa	Yaa Asantewa was born in the early 19th century in the Ashanti region of Ghana. When her son, the Asantehene (king), was captured

by the British during their attempt to colonize the Ashanti region, she gave the people courage and led the fight to defend their land, culture, and way of life.

Asar — The Kemetic (Ancient Egyptian) Ntr (deity) made up one-third of the original Trinity, the Afrikan Trinity, which was comprised of a Father, Mother, and Child (the Afrikan Family(, instead of a Father, Son, and masculine Holy Ghost. He was the first known "Crucified Savior". The Greeks renamed him Osiris.

ASCAC — The Association for the Study of Classical African Civilizations, an international umbrella organization of study groups dedicated to the re-ascension of Afrika.

Ase — A Yoruba word (pronounced ah-shay) that means "amen." It is the response frequently used by the people in the Call-and-Response form of the Libation.

Aset — The Kemet (Ancient Egyptian) Ntr (deity) who made up the female third of the Afrikan trinity. She was known to the Greeks as Isis (see Asar).

Asili A term used by Dr. Marimba Ani in her book, Yurugu, which describes the essence and ideological core of a culture. It is the matrix of a cultural entity. It must be identified and understood in order to make sense of the collective creations (including behaviors) of the members of that culture.

Ausa The ethnic group of Afrikan Americans. The "peculiar" institution of enslavement created one people out of dozens, if not hundreds of ethnic groups kidnapped from Afrika. While Afrikan Americans may have ancestors who are Asante, Yoruba, or Menda, *they* are not Asante, Yoruba, or Mende. During the almost 400 years of our presence in North and South America, Afrikan Americans have been melded into a new people, the Ausa *(Afrikans from the United States of America)*, who have a proud heritage of resistance and creative genius.

Axiology The governing nature of relationships.

Baba A word from the ki-Swahili language of East Afrika that means "father". It is also used as a title, especially for a religious leader.

Barnett

Ida B. Wells Barnett was born in Mississippi in 1862. She was a gifted journalist. She displayed a love of truth and courage when she became famous as an anti-lynching crusader and continued to write about lynching despite threats and actual attacks on her. She was thrown off a moving train by a white conductor and other white men when she refused to give up her seat on the train to a white person. She died in 1931.

Beaty

Mario Beaty is the International President of ASCAC. He is a learned Egyptologist who has mastered reading and interpreting the mdw ntr (hieroglyphics). He is on the faculty of Howard University in Washington, D.C.

Bethune

Mary McLeod Bethune was born in 1875 in Mayesville, South Carolina, the youngest of seventeen children born to sharecroppers. She had a burning desire for and achieved an education after great sacrifice, hard work, and perseverance. Organized Bethune College (now Bethune-Cookman University) in a Daytona Beach, FL garbage dump. She became an advisor to many organizations and to an American president. She died in 1955

Bindele — Word used by the Lunda-Luvale ethnic group of Northern Zimbabwe which described a modern ailment resulting from possession of the Afrikan psyche by European culture, values, and history.

Browder — Anthony Browder is a brilliant Afrikan Centered scholar who has done excellent research and who has written profoundly important books. He is the first AUSA to fund and participate in an Archeological dig in Kemet.

Carr — Greg Kimathi Carr is a brilliant scholar born in Nashville, TN. He is an attorney, chair of the Africana Studies Department at Howard University in Washington, D.C., a captivating lecturer, and an excellent teacher. He is first vice president of ASCAC.

Carver — George Washington Carver, called "The Wizard of Tuskegee", was born in Diamond Grove, Missouri, in 1864. He was an agricultural scientific genius who discovered

325 uses for the peanut, 118 uses for the sweet potato, and seventy-five products from the pecan. He extracted many dyes and paints from Alabama dirt and made hundreds of useful products from waste material like corn stalks and excess cotton. He walked in the woods almost every day and said that the plants told him how to best use them. He died in 1943.

Clarke

Dr. John Henrik Clarke was the intellectual son of brilliant but under-recognized scholars like Hubert Henry Harrison and Arthur Schomburg; the intellectual brother of John G. Jackson and Yosef ben-Jochannon and the intellectual father of giants such as Asa G. Hilliard, Marimba Ani and Wade W. Nobles.

Classical

This is a term used in the Western world to describe anything that is original, old, and makes up the standard for that area. As an example, the term "classical music" describes the music of early Europe without even mentioning Europe and negates the music of other cultures even though they may be older and even more influential.

Conscious	The state of awareness of identity, purpose, and direction from a cultural standpoint.
Cosmology	The way a people or culture looks at the universe, including its history, structure, and everything in it. It is the way they answer the question, "How did I get here?"
Carruthers	Dr. Jacob Carruthers was a cutting-edge intellectual warrior-leader who was a founding member and first president of ASCAC. He was a co-founder of the Kemetic Institute at Northeastern University and co-founded the Kemetic Institute in Chicago.
Culture	The totality of thought and practice by which a people create itself and presents itself to history and humanity. It has been said to represent the behavior and habits of one's Ancestors.
Cultural Misorientation	A psychological paradigm, created by Dr. Kobi Kambon, former Chair of the Department of Psychology at the Florida A & M University in Tallahassee, FL that asserts that for any Afrikan person to behave and function like a European or European American is mentally abnormal and represents a

psychiatric/psychological disorder. See bindele.

Declarations of Innocence These were affirmations that the ancient Afrikans of Kemet (ancient Egypt) had to truthfully recite after death in order to be admitted into paradise or the next ideal state of existence. They were recited by the deceased in the presence of the Ntrs (aspects of the Creator) and the Ancestors, and if the deceased was truthful, he or she was taken to the father by the Son in the presence of the Mothers. See the chapter on Afrikan values.

Delany Martin Delany was born "free" in 1812 in Charles Town, Virginia, now known as Charleston, West Virginia. He was also a multi-genius and learned to read even though it was against the law for Afrikans to read. In 1834, he started an organization called the Philanthropic Society, which is believed to be the foundation of the Underground Railroad. He started his own newspaper, The Mystery, in 1843. He was a physician and was very proud of his dark complexion and other Afrikan features. He wrote two books on Ethnology and is called "The

Father of Black Nationalism because he believed that Afrikans in America needed to work together to make themselves and Afrika strong economically, militarily, and politically. He believed that Afrikans in America needed to emigrate (leave America) if they were to reach their potential of greatness. He was a novelist, lecturer, abolitionist. And was the first Black officer in the U.S. Army. After the Civil War, he lived in Charleston, SC, where he served as customs inspector and trial justice. He died in 1885 in Xenia, Ohio.

Dessalines

John-Jacques Dessalines was born in the 18th century in Afrika and was kidnapped and taken to Haiti where he was enslaved. He had virtual freedom of movement because he was feared by his "master." He was second in command to Toussaint L'Ouverture during the initial part of the Haitian revolution. He became commander of the rebel armies when Toussaint was tricked into a French prison and successfully completed the revolution, defeating the best and strongest army in Europe at the time. He had the clarity of vision to remind his troops and the people that race was the primary cause of the conflict and that they should fight for racial pride.

Didactic	The science of instruction generally refers to formal lectures.
Diop	Cheikh Anta Diop was a Brilliant Senegalese researcher, writer, anthropologist, nuclear physics, and all-around multi-genius who did work that definitively proved that the Kamites or Kamieu (ancient Egyptians) were Black.
Direction	Methods that you use to achieve your purpose in a positive or negative manner.
Dr. Ben	Dr. Yosef ben-Jochannon was a scholar–warrior who studied and led educational tours to Egypt for many years. He wrote and self-published several books on the African aspect of Egypt's history and the Afrikan origins of religion.
Drew	Charles Drew was born in 1904 in Washington D.C. He excelled in many areas, including athletics, research, scholarship, and surgery. He was Chief Surgeon and chief of staff at Freedman's Hospital (now Howard University Hospital) in Washington, D.C. He discovered

methods of preserving blood plasma in what are now called "blood banks" (which are found in most large hospitals), which has saved the lives of untold millions of people. He died in North Carolina in 1950 after having an automobile accident.

DuBois — William Edward Burghardt DuBois was a brilliant scholar, activist, social scientist, and Pan-Afrikanist who did work that still retains its relevance today.

DuBois — Shirley Graham Dubois was the second wife of W.E.B. DuBois and was a writer and activist. She was the founding director of Ghana Television and introduced Malcolm X to Kwame Nkrumah

Environmental racism — This term describes the practice of dumping or storing hazardous materials in communities of Black and Brown people.

Egypt — The name given to the Northeast nation of the Afrikan continent originally called Kemet by its original inhabitants. The term arose from the mispronunciation by the Greeks of Kemetic words.

Ethnic group	A group of people who share a common culture, language, religion, and ancestry.
Ethos	The fundamental values peculiar to a specific culture or group of people.
Fante	An ethnic group found mostly in the eastern coastal area of Ghana, West Afrika. They are part of the Akan group of people. They are also called Fanti.
Finch	Charles Finch is a brilliant physician/scholar formerly on the faculty of Morehouse Medical School in Atlanta, GA. He has studied ancient Egypt and its language (mdw ntr or hieroglyphics). He has written several very important books that should be studied by all people who are interested in Afrikan Centered thought.
Ga	One of the four main ethnic groups of Ghana, West Afrika. Their original home is the area now known as Accra, Ghana's capital city.
Garvey	Hon. Marcus Mosiah Garvey was born in Jamaica in 1887. He Be-lieved in "Africa for the Africans"

that all Africans should return to Africa from wherever they found themselves in order to rebuild Africa and make it great again. Garvey led the most successful mass movement of the African American masses in the history of America. He made powerful enemies among the Negro bourgeois and intelligentsia, but some (W.E.B. DuBois) later regretted their opposition to him. He formed a successful (for a while) nursing corps, newspaper, shipping line, and factory corporation. He was imprisoned for mail fraud for two years, starting in 1925. He died a lonely and disappointed man in London in 1940.

Genocide — The process of killing all of a particular race or ethnic group. It has also been called "ethnic cleansing".

Ghana — Two definitions: (1) Ghana was the first of the medieval West Afrikan empires lasting from the seventh century to the 13th century. It was located in the area that is now part of Mauritania and Mali. (2) Ghana is a West Afrikan country, formerly known as the Gold Coast, which was the first Afrikan country to

	declare independence from colonial control in 1957 under Kwame Nkrumah, a Pan Afrikanist.
Gottengen	German university that according to Martin Bernal in *Black Athena* originated the idea that the Greeks were the source of all wisdom and philosophy.
Habari Gani	A ki-Swahli term that means, "What's the News?" or "What's Happening?"
Hall	Prince Hall was born in slavery in 1735, probably in the West Indies. In 1776, he urged the Massachusetts legislature to free all enslaved Afrikans. In 1787, Hall founded Afrikan Lodge #459, the oldest Afrikan social organization in America and prototype for today's Black Masons. In 1797, he forced Boston to provide schools for "Free" Afrikans.
Hilliard	Asa G. Hilliard, III, one of the great scholar-warriors of Afrikan Centered thought. His books are ALL must-reads.
Heru	The child in the Afrikan Trinity. He was the son of Asar and Aset.

Harambee	A Ki-Swahili word that means "pull together." It is used in Rites of Passage as a way of leaving the concept of unity on the minds of the trainers and trainees when separating for the day.
Identity	Who you are. How you feel about the real you and the people who are connected to you. How others see you based upon what you do in life.
Ideology	The body of ideas reflecting the social needs and aspirations of a group or culture.
Igbo	An ethnic group of southeastern Nigeria. It is one of the "Big Three" or three largest ethnic groups of Nigeria. Also spelled "Ibo" and is pronounced"Ee-boe".
Imhotep	Born in Kemet (ancient Egypt) during one of the Golden Ages of Afrikan people almost 5000 years ago, he was a multigenius and excelled in several areas: He was a sage (a person of great wisdom), a scribe (a person who wrote and rewrote many books for people to read), a philosopher (a person who can evaluate things without depending on other people's opinions – he did listen to other

people, however), an astronomer (he was very familiar with the solar system and knew that the world was round thousands of years ago), a vizier (a prime minister who advised the king), and a priest (he was the chief priest). He was an architect and master builder. He designed and built the world's first pyramid, the step pyramid at Saqqara in Egypt. He was the first known physician and knew anatomy, pharmacology, and surgery.

Jackson — John G. Jackson, a native of Aiken, SC, was a brilliant scholar who wrote several profoundly important books. His work is basic in understanding Afrikan Centered thought.

James — George G. M. James was a Guyanese-born scholar of Greek antiquities who authored the seminal book, *Stolen Legacy: The Greeks Were Not the Authors of Greek Philosophy, But the. People of North Africa Commonly Called the Egyptians.*

Jeffries — The last name of two superb warrior-scholars in the Afrikan Centered movement. Drs Leonard and Rosaland Jeffries are brilliant scholars, historians, researchers, and lecturers.

Jegna

Jegna is an Ethiopian concept suggested by Dr. Wade Nobles to take the place of Mentor, a Greek character. Nobles states that a Jegna is a person who:

- Has been tested in struggle or battle
- Has demonstrated extraordinary and unusual fearlessness
- Has determination and courage in protecting his/her people, land, and culture
- Has shown diligence and dedication to Afrikan people
- Produces exceptionally high-quality work
- Has dedicated themselves to the protection, defense, nurturance, and development of our young by advancing our people, place, and culture.

Karenga

Maulana Karenga is a brilliant scholar, author, Pan-Afrikan activist, college professor who is the creator of the Afrikan American holiday, Kwanzaa.

Kemet

One of the main names for the Northeastern Afrikan nation now called Egypt. It was the longest-lasting country in history, having survived more than three thousand years. The word was spelled Kmt and meant, "The Land (or Community) of the Blacks". The people were called Kamiru or Kamites.

King Martin Luther King, Jr. was born in 1929 in Atlanta, Georgia. He was a courageous minister and a major "Civil Rights" leader. His career had two periods, and we remember the first period mostly, which included the "March on Washington" and his two most remembered speeches. The second period, which probably caused his death, was marked by his efforts to improve the lives of Afrikan Americans as well as poor and powerless people of all races and get them more economic and political power. He was killed by a cowardly sniper in Memphis, Tennessee in 1968.

King Richard King was a psychiatrist from Los Angeles. He has done major work on the pigment melanin and has written extensively on that topic. He was a prime mover in the series of lectures that occurred throughout the country in the 1990s called "Melanin Conferences".

Lebby — Larry Lebby was an excellent artist who was born in Dixiana, SC. His work is well-known worldwide.

Libation — A ceremony in which the Ancestors are formally asked to join the living in the effort being attempted. It is a way of honoring them while asking them to honor us with their presence.

Maafa — Ki-Swahili word, which means great disaster. It was first used by Dr. Marimba Ani to describe the colonization and enslavement process, including the Middle Passage (Ani, 1997).

Principles of MAAT — The Kamites believed that God was so great that mere man could not begin to comprehend an entity that could create life. Humans then attempted to become God-like by attempting to understand the aspects of God and respecting all of God's creations. Maat was the Kemetic female wisdom principle. The principles of Maat (Truth, Justice, Righteousness, Harmony, Balance, Order, Propriety, and Reciprocity) underlay all of the ideas about divine nature and human relations. All people tried to live by these principles.

Maroons — Afrikans who escaped from slavery and established settlements away from slavery in Jamaica, America, Surinam, Brazil, and wherever the kidnapped and enslaved Afrikans were taken.

Mbongi — A Kikongo concept that describes an organization of people or groups that come together to make plans for specific situations or to solve problems

Mdw Nfr — Kemetic term meaning "Good Speech".

Mdr Ntr — Kemetic term meaning "Divine Speech". It was called "hieroglyphics" by the ancient Greeks.

Mentacide — A term coined by psychologist Bobby Wright that described the minds of Black people affected by white supremacy.

Middle Passage — The leg of the triangular trip of enslavement that started in Afrika and ended in the Caribbean or the east coast of America.

Middleton	Listervelt Middleton was a brilliant scholar-poet-warrior in Columbia, SC, whose groundbreaking ETV program, "For The People," introduced many of the Afrikan Centered scholars to the masses of Afrikan people in America. His crystal clear vision and uncompromising scholarship make his poetry timeless.
Netcher (Ntr)	The personification of one of the divine principles of the Creator. The aspects of God around us (nature).
NABSW	National Association of Black Social Workers. A Pan Afrikan organization
Nana	A title of respect used by Akan people, especially the Asante, which refers to elders and also to those with royal blood.
Nationalism	A philosophy in which races or ethnic groups seek the freedom or ability to tule themselves, to have sovereignty.
Netcher (Ntr)	The Kamites (or Kamieu) believed that God was so great that mere man could not begin to comprehend an entity that could create life. Humans then attempted to become God-like by attempting

to understand the aspects of God and respecting all of God's creations. Ntrs were the personification of the divine of the Creator. They are the aspects of God that are around us (nature).

Nobles — Wade W. Nobles is a brilliant experimental social psychologist who is a founding member of the Association of Black Psychologists and who is the author of several very important books.

Nguzo Saba — The Seven Principles of Kwanza: Umoja (Unity), Kugichagulia (Self Definition), Ujima, Ujamaa, Nia, Kuumba, Imani.

Ontology — The nature of the way reality is perceived by a people.

Pan Afrikan — The recognition that all people of Afrikan descent throughout the world are the same and should be joined together by political and economic ties as well as racial and cultural ones.

Project: Sankofa — An Afrikan Centered Rites of Passage Program, originating in Columbia, South Carolina.

Purpose — Your reason for being on this earth. What you are really trying to do.

Race	A social construct created by whites in Western Europe tried to separate the "types" of humanity in a fashion that created superior and inferior.
Racism	A belief that one's own race is superior and allowing that feeling to cause discrimination and antagonism against those other races.
Reparations	Compensation for generations of forced labor that benefitted others and for organized discrimination, which provided obstacles to the attainment of generational wealth.
Rites of Passage	A formalized method of helping a person move smoothly from one stage of life to another.
Sanchez	Poet, scholar, and activist on the faculty of Temple University
Sankofa	A Ghanaian concept that means, literally, "Go back and fetch it." It is represented by a bird with its head turned back so that it is looking back behind itself. Sankofa means that we cannot move forward into a meaningful future without having a knowledge and understanding of the past.

Self-concept	How one defines self. Self-concept deals with who you are. It deals with your group identity.
Self-esteem	How one feels about oneself. Self-esteem deals with how you feel about who you are. It deals with individual identity.
Small	James Small, a native of Georgetown, South Carolina, taught at the City College of New York for many years and has led multiple educational tours to Afrika. He is a brilliant lecturer and expert on Afrikan spiritual systems.
Stockholm Syndrome	A psychological phenomenon in which hostages, captives, or enslaved persons bond with their captors or enslavers and become sympathizers and supporters.
Tribe	One way of seeing tribe is as a kinship group, but it has been used to detrimentally describe people of color such as Afrikans and Native Americans, while Europeans who fit the same definition are called ethnic groups.
Twiggs	An excellent Batik artist, Leo Twiggs was born in South Carolina

and is a retired professor of art, South Carolina State University, Orangeburg, SC.

Utamaroho — The vital force or energy source of a culture. It gives a culture its emotional tone and activates the collective behavior of the members of that culture. It is born out of the asili and also affirms the asili. It is also a manifestation of the asili. (Ani, 1994)

Utamawazo — Culturally structured thought. It is the way that a culture influences its members to think. It is also born out of the asili but also fulfills the asili. It is a manifestation of the asili. (Ani, 1994)

Van Sertima — Guyanese-born historian and professor at Rutgers University who has authored or edited many extremely important books.

Watkins-Beaty — Valethia Watkins Beaty is a brilliant scholar-teacher with expertise in women's issues from an Afrikan Centered perspective. She is on the faculty of Howard University in Washington, DC.

Welsing — Frances Cress Welsing was a theoretical psychiatrist who formulated the Cress Theory of Racism/White Supremacy.

White privilege — Unearned privilege based on race rather than merit.

Williams — Dr. Chancellor Williams is the author of one of the most informative and important books written.

Williams — Dr. Daniel Hale Williams was born in Pennsylvania in 1858. Because Afrikan American physicians could not get hospital privileges, he created and established Provident Hospital in Chicago so that all physicians would be able to practice their profession. Organized Freedman's Hospital (now Howard University Hospital) into departments and stimulated the start of the first nursing school for Afrikan Americans. Performed the first known successful surgery on the heart in this country. Died in Chicago in 1931.

Wilson — Amos Wilson was a brilliant theoretical psychologist, college professor, and author whose works are necessary reading for anyone interested in psychology or Pan-Afrikan thought.

Woodson — Carter G. Woodson, born in Canton, Virginia in 1875, is called the "Father of Negro History" because he developed and started the celebration of "Negro History Week," which later became "Black History Month." He aggressively and uncompromisingly believed that Afrikans in America could make no positive progress until everyone knew and internalized their true history. He organized the Association for the Study of Negro (now Black) Life and History. He organized two journals, one for research for scholars and the other designed to teach the public. He died in 1950.

Worldview — The way a people understand their surroundings and make sense of life and the universe.

Yoruba — An ethnic group in Nigeria.

Yurugu — The title of an extremely important book written by Dr. Marimba Ani.

X — Malcolm X, was born Malcolm Little in Omaha, Nebraska on May 19, 1925. Both parents were Black Nationalist followers of Hon. Marcus M. Garvey. His father was murdered by white racists when Malcolm was six years old. He believed that Afrikans worldwide should have the right to defend themselves, and for this, he was branded as a person who preached violence. X had to make at least two very difficult choices in his life based on his value system: (1) The choice to leave the criminal life and become a Muslim follower of Hon. Elijah Muhammad and (2) The choice to leave The Nation of Islam when he discovered what he considered to be ethical and moral problems in that Religion/ Philosophy. A study of his life reveals that he not only believed strongly in the Afrikan values that have been discussed (Maat and the Virtues, especially) but was able to base his loyalty on his values and dared to follow through in his actions.

Appendix A

Black Men on Which to Do Biographical Research

Note: Each of these names exemplifies one or more of the values, principles, and virtues mentioned in Unit Three. Information about some of these men may be difficult to find but will be well worth the look. Some of these men may have done the right thing for the "wrong" reasons and vice versa, but their lives are believed to be instructive to our youth. This research may also be used as an optional part of Unit Three if the group of trainees is progressing and growing appropriately. However, if one trainee is given extra work, all must be given extra work.

Narmer

Jacque Dessalines

Imhotep

Chevalier de St. Georges

William Monroe Trotter

Edward Wilmot Blyden

Martin Delany

Paul Robeson

Henry McNeal Turner

Benjamin E. Mays

Richard Allen

John A. Russwurm

Askia the Great

Chaka

Hannibal of Carthage

Cetewayo

Frederick Douglass

Henry Highland Garnet

George Washington Carver

Alexander Crummell

Adam Clayton Powell, Jr.

Carter G. Woodson

Prince Hall

Malcolm X

Ahmed Baba

Garrett A. Morgan

Martin Luther King, Jr.

Robert Smalls

Charles Drew

Hubert Henry Harrison

George A.P. Bridgetower

Denmark Vesey

John Henrik Clarke

Chancellor Williams

Monroe Work

Jacob Carruthers

Haki Madhubiti

Elijah McCoy

Daniel Hale Williams

Booker T. Washington

Granville T. Woods

David Walker

Jan Ernst Matzeliger

Samuel Coleridge-Taylor

Paul Cuffe

Josef ben-Jochannon

John G. Jackson

Asa G. Hilliard, III

George G. M. James

Appendix B

Black Women on Which to Do Biographical Research

Note: Each of these names exemplifies one or more of the values, principles, or virtues studied in Unit Three. Some of this information may be difficult to find but is well worth the look. If the trainees are progressing better than anticipated, some of these may be given as elective additional research assignments. If one trainee is given extra work, all must be given extra work.

Nzinga	Sojourner Truth
Tiye	Hatshetsut
Maggie L. Walker	Harriet Ross Tubman
Madame C.J. Walker	Ida B. Wells Barnett
Mary Church Terrell	Mary McLeod Bethune
Gwendolyn Brooks	Zora Neale Hudson
Nannie Helen Burroughs	Dorothy Height
Winnie Mandela	Wilma Rudolph
Frances Cress Welsing	Charshee McIntyre
Dona Marimba Richards	Lorraine Hansberry
Queen Candace of Ethiopia	Yaa Asantewa
Toni Morrison	Charlotte Forten

Sonia Sanchez

Dorothy Height

Modjeska Monteith Simkins

Anna Julia Cooper

Amy Jacques Garvey

Audrey Lorde

Maria Stewart

Shirley Chisholm

Barbara Sizemore

Audley (Queen Mother) Moore

Rosa Parks

Nikki Giovanni

Septima Clark

Nehanda

Daisy Bates

Makeda

Fannie Lou Hamer

Mary Ellen Pleasant

Mae C. Jemison

Appendix C

Proverbs that can be used in Rites of Passage Programs

Many concepts are best taught by proverbs, sayings that have meanings that go beyond the superficial words. Our Afrikan Ancestors used proverbs frequently, and many books have been written that list many Afrikan proverbs. The sayings below are taken from various sources, including Shakespeare and the Christian Bible. They have been very useful to us in stimulating abstract thought towards thinking "outside the box".

"One cannot both feast and become rich." (Asante)

"When you follow in the path of your father, you learn to walk like him." (Asante)

"When you know who his friend is, you know who he is." (Senegal)

"Two birds disputed about a kernel when a third swooped down and carried it off."

"Do not mend your neighbor's fence before looking to your own."

The ruin of a nation begins in the homes of its people."

"A white dog does not bite another white dog."

"The fool speaks; the wise man listens."

"Too much discussion means an argument."

"There is no phrase without a double meaning."

"No one tests the depths of a river with both feet."

"Singing 'Hallelulia' everywhere does not prove piety."

"Don't be so much in love that you can't tell when the rain comes."

"One finger alone cannot kill even a louse."

"Do not call to a dog with a whip in your hand."

"A roaring lion kills no game."

"When life gives you lemons, make lemonade."

"Anything worth doing at all is worth doing well."

"Beauty is only skin deep."

"Pretty is as pretty does."

"A hard head makes a soft butt."

"The squeaky wheel gets the oil."

"You make your bed; you have to lay in it."

"You reap what you sow."

"You can't miss what you can't measure."

"When a job is first begun, never stop until it's done."

"Service is the rent that we must pay for life."

"You can catch more flies with honey than you can with vinegar."

"An ounce of prevention is worth a pound of cure."

"Always shoot for the sun, for if you miss, you'll still be among the stars."

"Don't burn your bridges behind you."

"When the going gets tough, the tough get going."

"Handle her/him with a long-handled spoon."

"A penny saved is a penny earned."

"Stand for something, or you'll fall for anything."

"What goes around, comes around."

"A good name is better than great riches."

"Your family is thrust upon you, but you choose your friends."

"To have a friend, you must be a friend."

"A bird in the hand is worth two in the bush."

"Luck is being prepared for opportunity."

"Practice makes perfect."

Appendix D

List of Words, Phrases, and Concepts

List of Words, Phrases, or Concepts Used During the Training That May Be Researched Electively or Independently by the Trainees

Ankh

Sankofa

Underground Railroad

Negro Convention Movement

Civil Rights Movement

Black Nationalism

Chattel Slavery

Middle Passage

Maafa

Pharaoh

Kemet

Slave Revolts

Maat

Civil War (participations of Afrikans in the military)

Haitian Revolution

Delayed gratification/sacrifice

Investing

Ancient Ghana

Mali

Songhay

Hausa States

Nubia/Nubians

Colonization

Emigration Society

The Harlem Renaissance

Maat

Afrikan Spirituality

History of the Association for the Study of Classical African Civilizations

History of the National Association of Black Social Workers

History of the Association of Black Psychologists

Palmares

Maroons

Afrikan Music

Mystery System of Kemet

The Osirian Drama

The Value of History

Notes

About the Authors

L-R: Baba Derrick Jackson, Dr. Burnett Kwadwo Gallman, Nana Joe E. Benton (Maa Kheru)

Joe Benton (Maa Kheru), a native of Seattle, Washington, had conceptualized, planned, organized, and implemented human service programs with an emphasis on youth for more than 40 years. Born in Chattanooga, Tennessee and raised in Seattle, Washington, he earned a B.A. Degree from Benedict College in Columbia, an M.S.W. from the University of Washington in Seattle, and did further study at the Wharton School of Business at the University of Pennsylvania. He taught psychology, history and sociology at the Columbia Junior College (now South University). He also did intensive study of history at the University of Bristol in Bristol, England.

More than three hundred troubled boys and girls have graduated from Mr. Benton's African Centered Manhood and Womanhood programs at St. Luke's Center and elementary and middle schools in the Columbia, SC area. Mr. Benton was a writer and a teacher of psychology, history, economics, and sociology at Columbia Junior College. He lectured nationally and did volunteer work in his spare time.

He was the 11th National president of the National Association of Black Social Workers, the first chairperson of the Board of the Organization of Afrikan Unity of South Carolina. He served for five years as the Special Assistant to the Bishop of the 7th Episcopal District of the AME Church.

He was married and the father of two and took great pride in his four grandchildren.

Derrick Jackson, a native of Harlem, NY, is an ordained priest who completed his indoctrination into the Priesthood with a special concentration on Afrikan and AUSA cultural and religious institutions. He is Senior Pastor at KRST Universal Temple, an Afrikan-centered religious institution that uses ancient wisdom texts featuring the Gospel according to ancient Kemet as its foundation.

Jackson completed the course of study at the Cooper-Lewter Institute for study, application, and advancement of Soul Therapy and its four aspects: Biological-Psychological-Sociological and Spiritual Development. He is a community activist and Afrikan historian who has served in many capacities in many community organizations, including Bridge Builders, A Concerned Group of Men, Midlands Primary Health Care Association, Bible Way Social Action Foundation, and Our Community Organization.

He is a graduate of Midwestern States University and was formerly employed at the Richland Memorial Hospital in Columbia in the Department of Transfusion Services, specializing in blood banking and immunohematology.

Mr. Jackson serves as a lecturer and consultant on Classical Afrikan History and Rites of Passage Programs. He has worked extensively with at-risk youth and has participated in developing the St. Lukes Manhood and Womanhood programs.

He is married and is the father of one daughter.

Burnett Gallman has participated in the positive development of many young people through the years through direct mentoring, Rites of Passage Programs, and the development of a shadowing program in which young people spend their summers following him around during the workday.

A native of Hartsville, SC, he is a graduate of Benedict College in Columbia, SC and Hahnemann Medical School (now Drexel Medical University) in Philadelphia, PA. He is retired from the private practice of Gastroenterology and Internal Medicine and is currently employed full time as a Gastroenterologist at the Columbia Veterans Administration Hospital.

He has taught Junior High School Science and taught Afrikan and Afrikan American history at the Columbia Junior College (now South University)

He has authored or co-authored five books and is a member of the National Board of the Association for the Study of Classical African Civilizations, the current chairperson of the board of the Organization of Afrikan Unity of South Carolina and is involved in disseminating information about health issues as well as historical and cultural issues through writing and several radio programs as well as lectures.

He is married and the father of one daughter.